IN KINDLING FLAME

IN KINDLING FLAME

The Story of Hannah Senesh
1921-1944

LINDA ATKINSON

Lothrop, Lee & Shepard Books
New York

For my children Willie and Sara,
my blessings.

Hazak v'ematz.

Hannah Senesh's poems and excerpts from her diary, her correspondence with her mother and brother, and written recollections of Catherine Senesh, Yoel Palgi, and Reuven Dafne are from *Hannah Senesh: Her Life and Diary* by Hannah Senesh. Copyright © 1966 by Hakibbutz Publishing House, Ltd. English edition copyright © 1971 by Nigel Marsh. Reprinted by permission of Schocken Books, Inc. and Vallentine Mitchell & Co., Ltd., London, England. *Hannah Senesh: Her Life and Diary* is available in the United States from Schocken Books, Inc.

Library of Congress Cataloging in Publication Data

Atkinson, Linda.
In kindling flame.

Includes index.
Summary: A biography of a Jewish heroine whose resistance work during World War II made her a martyr and an inspiration to those with whom she worked.
1. Senesh, Hannah, 1921–1944—Juvenile literature. 2. Holocaust, Jewish (1939–1945)—Hungary—Juvenile literature. 3. World War, 1939–1945— Underground movements, Jewish—Hungary—Juvenile literature. 4. Jews— Palestine—Biography—Juvenile literature. [1. Senesh, Hannah, 1921–1944. 2. Jews—Biography. 3. Holocaust, Jewish (1939–1945)—Hungary. 4. World War, 1939–1945—Underground movements, Jewish—Hungary. 5. Hungary—History— 1918–1945] I. Title. CT1919.P38S363   1984
940.53′15′03924[92]   83-24392 ISBN 0-688-02714-8

Printed in the United States of America.

FIRST EDITION

1 2 3 4 5 6 7 8 9 10

Book design and calligraphy by Carole Lowenstein

Acknowledgments

"Jews! Write it down! Write it down!"

SIMON DUBNOW, HISTORIAN AND JEW,
JUST BEFORE HE WAS SHOT BY NAZIS
IN LATVIA, 1942.

The subject of the Holocaust is a terrible subject, and one from which I, an American Jew, stayed away for many years, sensing that I would not be able to deal with the things I would find there. Writing this book has, indeed, brought me face to face with such things. But it has also enabled me to understand what the Jews of Europe in their agony understood, the moving spirit behind Dubnow's haunting injunction: making the truth known is in itself an act of resistance and of restitution. For giving me the opportunity to add my writing to the record, and for her commitment to this project from the beginning, I will always be grateful to Dorothy Briley, Editor-in-Chief, Lothrop, Lee & Shepard Books.

It is a pleasure to thank my editor, Sharon L. Steinhoff, for the skill, dedication and good spirit with which she worked on this book. I would also like to thank the staff of The Leo Baeck Institute, and Marek Web and Fruma Moehrer of the YIVO Institute for Jewish Research. Special thanks are due Esther Togman, librarian and archivist of the Zionist Archives and Library of New York for being unfailingly kind and helpful; Katalin L. Vida of the Corvina Press of Budapest, for her cheerful support; Elisabeth Marton, the former Baronness Böske Hatvany, for her careful reading and her kind consideration; my friend Gudrun Fonfa, for helping me think things through. Finally, I would like to thank my mother, Sara Nathanson Goldenberg, who read this book in manuscript form during one very hot August. Her faith in my work meant more than words can say.

This book would not be possible, however, without the gracious support of George Senesh, for which I offer my humblest thanks. I hope this book justifies his confidence and trust in me.

LINDA ATKINSON
Brooklyn, New York
March 1984

Contents

PART TWO: 1944

PART THREE: 1945 and After

PART ONE

1935-1944

CHAPTER 1

1935

"We'll meet...
ten years from now!"

THE roar of the airplane made it impossible for them to talk. They sat silently, stiffly, weighed down by their weapons, their parachutes, their bulky winter clothing. In forty minutes, they would be over Yugoslavia, and the first part of their mission would begin.

There were four of them. Reuven, Yonah, Abba and Hannah. Four young Jews on their way to Hitler's Europe. Each of them had been born there, in quieter times. Each had escaped and found safety in Palestine. But now, on the thirteenth of March, 1944, they were going back. Trained to fight by the British in the deserts of Palestine and Egypt, taught to use weapons, parachutes, radio transmitters, they were going back to gather information for the British about German defenses, to establish escape routes for captured Allied airmen and to rescue as many Jews as they could.

The airplane buzzed and shook its way through the black night sky. Reuven studied the faces of the others: Abba and Yonah, deep in thought; Hannah, her blue eyes calm and clear.

At twenty-two, Hannah was the youngest member of the crew, the only woman, and the only one who was positive that the mission would succeed. When she saw Reuven looking at her, she smiled and gave him the "thumbs up" sign, her favorite sign for victory.

Years later, Reuven described Hannah as a "poet-tomboy," a "girl who dreamed of being a heroine, and who was a heroine." On the night of the mission, "her excitement was contagious," he wrote. "We were all infected by it. Gradually tension relaxed, and the air seemed lighter."

According to the plan, Reuven and Hannah were going to jump first. Then the plane would circle and make a second pass over the target so Yonah and Abba could jump. Once on the ground, they would meet with the Yugoslavian partisans and make their way on foot to the border with Hungary. The German occupation was about to begin, and close to a million Jews were still living there. One of them was Catherine Senesh, Hannah's mother.

"Mother Darling," Hannah had written just before boarding the plane for Yugoslavia. "In a few days I'll be so close to you

The city of Budapest divided by the river Danube.

—and yet so far. Forgive me, and try to understand. With a million hugs. Your Annie."

Hannah hadn't seen her mother since 1939, when she had left her native Budapest for Palestine. She had begged her mother to go with her then. Anti-Jewish feeling in Hungary was already high and rising. The dangers faced by Jews all over Europe were the worst in recent memory. But no matter what arguments Hannah brought to bear, her mother would not leave Budapest. Like most of her friends and relatives, Catherine believed that the wave of bad feelings against Jews would soon recede and things would be once again the way they had been when she was a girl.

The Budapest Opera House, one of the many magnificent buildings in Budapest, which was a great cultural center in the 1920s.

Budapest had been a wonderful place to live then, in the early years of the twentieth century. It had been a fairy-tale city of candle-lit palaces and elegant boulevards, an international city where European princes and American millionaires promenaded in the squares, gathered at the Opera, sat talking in the gilded coffeehouses until the early hours of the morning. Budapest had been a good place to live for people in the small but important middle class too, the comfortable members of the professions, the trades and business. And it was a very good place to live if you were a Jew. Like the states of Western Europe, to which Hungary was close in spirit if not geography, Hungary had emancipated the Jews during the nineteenth century, lifting the legal restrictions that until then had kept them separate from other people and outside of Hungarian life and culture. With emancipation, Jews had the same rights as other Hungarians, the same political and legal freedoms: They could live wherever they chose, travel wherever they wished, attend any schools, take up any occupation, own anything they liked, even land and weapons.

Anti-Semitism was not entirely gone from people's feelings, but by the end of the nineteenth century, it was less important and weaker than it had ever been. Jews, especially those in the cities (who had always been more worldly than those in the countryside), began to move outside the Jewish community and the institutions of Jewish culture, and participate in national politics as well as national and international culture. They began to travel and to write; they entered the arts in great numbers; they entered the sciences, the civil service, the professions. They found that they could assimilate, "fit in," with their non-Jewish neighbors if they tried. Though they might not be regarded as "quite the same" as other people, or "quite as Hungarian," their Jewishness was not the barrier it had once been. Some Jews, seeing that their Jewishness was being overlooked rather than accepted, resisted assimilation. But most urban Jews welcomed the opportunity and tried to minimize the ways in which they were different.

Both Catherine Senesh and her husband Bela were children of sophisticated, assimilated Jewish families. Bela had gone even further toward assimilation than his family by changing his name from the recognizably Jewish "Schlesinger" to the Hungarian-sounding "Senesh." He didn't do this in order to deny that he was a Jew. But, in keeping with his wish to "fit in," he wanted his

Catherine and Bela Senesh, 1920.

Jewishness to be a private matter, not the first thing people knew about him.

Bela Senesh was a man of great ambition and intensity. He had had rheumatic fever as a child, and had been told that he would not live a long life. Perhaps that accounted for his drive and energy. In 1912, while still a student in the university, he got a job as a newspaper reporter. In 1915, soon after graduation, he became a theater critic and then a writer of plays.

By 1921, when he was twenty-seven years old, Bela Senesh was a leading playwright and a regular columnist for one of Budapest's best newspapers. He had married the lovely Catherine Salzberger and purchased a grand old house in a tree-lined section of town. He and Catherine had a son, George, one year old, and a daughter, born on July 17 of that year, named Hannah.

Catherine, writing about those early years, remembered them as warm and happy, in spite of the fact that World War I had made anti-Semitism an active force in Hungary once again. The war left hundreds of thousands of people homeless, without money or jobs. It left the government in shambles. As the people suffered, old angers and old fears began to resurface. Jews, who had often in the past been used as scapegoats, found themselves again the subject of slander and suspicion.

Following the war, many political groups and parties struggled for power, but none of them was strong enough or popular enough to set things right. For a few months in 1919, the Communist Party took control of the Hungarian government. Led by a man named Bela Kun, this short-lived regime was overthrown in turn by people who wanted to bring the monarchy back to power. They considered the Communists traitors to Hungary. Because Kun was a Jew and because of the anti-Jewish feeling that already existed, all Jews were soon cast as traitors. They were singled out and blamed in ways they hadn't been for over fifty years. Universities established quotas to keep the number of Jewish students low. The police force established quotas too. So did the civil service. And in the countryside, gangs of thugs and ex-soldiers terrorized Jews, beating and murdering them in their

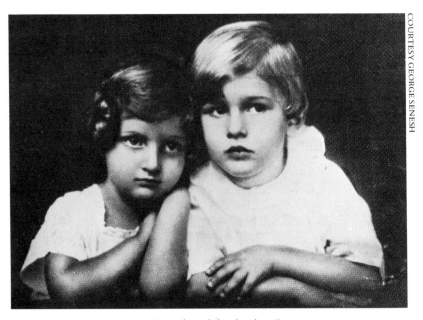

Young Hannah with her brother George.

homes, destroying their property, burning their crops. This violence was known as the White Terror, and no one in authority did anything to stop it.

Bela and Catherine Senesh, like most of the assimilated, educated Jews in Hungary's cities, were not directly affected by either the quotas or the violence. The situation troubled them, but it did not frighten them. They had a lively circle of friends, including both Christians and Jews, all of whom believed that the hard times facing the Jews would be over soon. Things had gone awry because of the war, they thought, but they would soon return to normal.

In addition to his work, Bela spent as much time as he could with his children. As Catherine later wrote, his children seemed especially precious to him and their time together was especially important since he knew he would probably not live to see them fully grown. Although he worked on his plays and essays in the evenings, sometimes late into the night, the mornings were reserved for George and Hannah. If he needed to rest, he took them on the bed with him and told them stories. When he could, he took them on outings to the park, the zoo and the paths beside the beautiful Danube River that divided Budapest into two parts. Sometimes in the afternoons, he held "story hours" for the children and their friends.

Then, in the spring of 1927, when George was seven and Hannah six, Bela died. Hannah didn't talk about her feelings then. But the sadness she felt came out in the poems she began to compose. One of them, a melancholy three lines, was written down and saved by her grandmother.

> I'd like to be glad but I don't know how
> No matter how I'd like to be
> No matter how I try to be.

In the fall, however, when Hannah started school, she seemed to blossom. We know from things she wrote years later that she thought about her father often, but that didn't make her moody

Four-year-old Hannah with her father and brother.

or withdrawn. If anything, it made her stronger and more active. She wanted to be like him. And according to her teachers, in her intelligence, good humor and talent, she was.

Hannah whizzed through the elementary grades at the top of her class although, her mother remembered, she never seemed to work at it. When she graduated in 1931, Catherine placed her in a widely respected girls' high school, which until that year had accepted only Protestants as students. Now the school accepted Jewish and Catholic girls too, though it required Jews to pay three times the standard tuition, and Catholics double.

Catherine went ahead with Hannah's application in spite of the tuition policy because she thought Hannah would thrive there —and she was right. Hannah loved the school, and she had a brilliant first year.

Armed with glowing reports from all Hannah's teachers, Catherine went to see the principal.

"In any other school, Hannah would have been awarded a scholarship," she said, recalling the conversation years later. "In this one I was paying a three-fold tuition fee. Because of this, regardless of how much I valued the high standards of the school, I said I felt compelled to enroll [my daughter] elsewhere."

At this "the teacher Hannah loved more than any other" spoke for her. "No, no," she said. "We won't allow her to leave. She is our finest student and sets an example to the entire school." The teacher organized support for Hannah, and her tuition was lowered from triple the usual fee to double.

Following the summer she turned thirteen, Hannah began to keep a diary. "This morning we visited Daddy's grave," she wrote in her first entry. Seven years had passed since Bela's death, but Hannah still felt close to him and proud of him. "I feel that even from beyond the grave Daddy is helping us," she wrote, "if in no other way than with his name. I don't think he could have left us a greater legacy."

School began again, and Hannah immersed herself in her studies and other activities with her usual enthusiasm. Sometimes weeks passed without a single diary entry. Then Hannah would

Hannah at age thirteen or fourteen.

explain that she had been extremely busy. Among other things she was working as a tutor after school.

"I don't think any other girl in my class earns as much," she wrote happily when she got a new student, a girl named Maria. "Now I can pay for dancing and skating lessons with my own money. Perhaps I'll even buy a season ticket for the ice rink."

Hannah was growing up, but while she was, the seeds of war were growing too. While Britain and France looked on nervously, weapons were being stockpiled in central Europe. In Hungary, there was talk of starting the draft again. Japan had just seized the vast Chinese province of Manchuria. In Italy, a dictator named Benito Mussolini had come to power, and in Germany, a man named Adolf Hitler.

"Mother says that the present atmosphere is very warlike," Hannah wrote in November 1934, after a national celebration in central Budapest. She was confused by events, and sometimes didn't know quite what to make of the military parades and shows of strength, like the one she had just witnessed. "I . . . thought that seeing them [the soldiers] on parade was beautiful," she wrote. Then, as if realizing what guns and tanks are really for, she became somber. "What would become of them in a war?" she wondered. "God protect us from war. Why, the whole world would be practically wiped out." With that she dropped the subject, as if it was something she just couldn't think about. "At the moment I have more immediate problems," she concluded. "Report time is approaching. It's possible I'll have a bad mark for neatness, but we'll hope for the best."

For the rest of the year, Hannah didn't mention war or politics at all. Instead, her diary is filled with news about her friends, school—she was ashamed of herself for finding French so difficult, despite having gotten an A in it—and the just "wonderful" things she did during the winter recess. There were long, quiet mornings at home, afternoons at the Ice Skating Club, and a big party given by the Dance Circle.

"I am rather jittery," she wrote the week before the party, "and wonder what it will be like. I have a lovely pink dress for the occasion." She knew that people didn't think she was a particularly pretty girl. "But," she wrote, "I hope I'll improve."

During that holiday, there were wonderful presents too: tickets to the opera (from her mother), two pairs of stockings (from her grandmother), ski socks (from her aunt Irma) and material for a summer dress (from her aunt Ilus). "And besides all this," Hannah wrote happily, "three handsome books."

Later in the spring, just before the end of the school term,

Hannah and her classmates planned a class reunion. In ten years, they decided, no matter where they were or what they were doing, they would come back to the school and have a party. Each girl got a ring with the reunion date engraved on it.

"We'll meet on May 1, 1945," Hannah wrote in great excitement. "Ten years from now! What a long time! How many things can happen before then."

How many things and what kinds of things, no one could have said. No one would have even guessed that the world would be changed completely by the time those ten years were over. And Hannah would be dead.

CHAPTER 2

1935-37

"I would like to be a great soul"

HANNAH'S high school years were rushing by, filled with things to do, books to read, people to meet, projects planned, begun, ended. A straight-A student from the beginning, she was soon tutoring a number of other students, participating in the Bible Society, the Literary Society, the Stenographic Circle. Summer days found her swimming and boating, winter vacations skiing and ice skating. By the time she was sixteen, she had become an excellent athlete, written three plays and nearly eighty poems, discovered spiritualism and astrology, become a vegetarian and given up vegetarianism, received two marriage proposals and five declarations of love. None were reciprocated.

"Mikki is coming again today," Hannah wrote about one boy. "It's a bit too much for me. We don't have enough in common and I find him rather shallow."

Gaby, another admirer, borrowed a book from Hannah and when he returned it, there was a photograph of himself inside. On it was written: "With love forever, Gaby."

"I didn't say a word about the picture," Hannah wrote in her diary. "Ever since, whenever I see him (quite often), he showers me with compliments, which I try to brush off."

Not all the boys who sought her out were greeted with such great indifference. But Hannah resisted what she saw as "the most common thing" among girls her age, the tendency to be totally preoccupied with boys and romance. In an entry made the summer she turned fourteen, Hannah conjured up her image of the "ideal boy": "He should be attractive and well dressed, but not a fop; he should be a good sportsman, but interested in other things besides sports; he should be cultured and intelligent, but good-humored, and not arrogant; and he should not chase after girls." Then she concluded abruptly, "So far I have not met a single boy like this."

Most of all, through her high school years, Hannah dreamed of being a writer. "It's my constant wish," she wrote when she was fifteen. "I don't know whether it's simply a desire for praise and fame, but I do know it is such a marvelous feeling to write something well that I think it is worth struggling to become a writer."

Sometimes she believed that she had talent, and sometimes she was filled with self-doubt. After one meeting of the Literary Society, at which she and her friend Agi read their poems, Hannah was very despondent. "I thought Agi's two poems were much better [than mine]," she wrote. "It somehow destroyed my confidence and interest in my own poems. . . . Agi is definitely more gifted."

But in spite of her ups and downs, she didn't stop wanting to be a writer and she never stopped working at it. "In a way I'm afraid to become too involved in writing, and in the idea that I am really talented," she wrote. "On the other hand, I can't stop writing, nor do I want to. . . . Goodness, it would be wonderful to be truly talented."

Alongside her wish to be a writer was her longing to be a truly exceptional person, " a great human being." Above-average people might suffer more than average people, she thought, but their joys were greater too. For her, the choice was easy. "I would like to be a great soul," she wrote. "If God will permit!"

There were moments however when Hannah found this longing difficult to accept. After expressing her wish in her diary, she noted, "What I wrote seems so terribly conceited. Big Soul! I am so far from anything like that. I'm just a struggling fifteen-year-old girl whose principal preoccupation is coping with herself."

Sometimes Hannah couldn't seem to do even that. She felt bothered and restless and couldn't figure out why. "For days I've been experiencing a general dissatisfaction with myself, and I don't know what's causing it," she wrote in April of her sixteenth year. "Nothing unusual has happened to me. And I've certainly done nothing wrong. I can't understand myself."

But no matter what conflicts engaged her, Hannah always rallied and her high spirits always returned. She was eager, inquiring, energetic, interested in everything she did. She read constantly and found many writers whose work she loved—Tolstoy and Dostoevsky among them. She enjoyed school, people, working hard, being busy.

"Except for drawing, I had all A's in my report," Hannah reported in February 1937. "Meanwhile, an important event: I got my first long party dress! It's blue taffeta, and everyone says I look very pretty in it. So far I've worn it only to the Hubermann concert, which was more noteworthy than my dress! The program consisted of Beethoven's *Spring Sonata,* the Bach *Sonata*, Brahms and Schubert."

That summer of 1937 Hannah toured Italy. It was her sixteenth summer, and she was on holiday in one of the most glorious countries of Europe. She loved everything about it. Lake Como, she wrote, was "a remarkable sight," its waters "now green, now blue, surrounded by snow-capped mountains." The train station in Venice was "in the middle of the sea," and the city itself was filled with "remarkably beautiful things." The little town of Menaggio, where she swam and played tennis, was "in one word: magnificent."

Sixteen-year-old Hannah's first long gown.

But the most moving experience of all occurred when Hannah visited the cathedral in Milan, a "story-book cathedral," she wrote, "resplendent, glittering. . . . Sacrificial candles burned on the altars, and the sun poured through some of the stained-glass windows."

After wandering through the rooms and vaults, Hannah took

the lift to the top of the dome and stepped outside. Her breath caught in her throat. "I was dazzled," she wrote. "The white marble sparkled under the blue sky and the entire scene reminded me of half-forgotten childhood fancies. This was how I had imagined fairyland to be: blue sky, white throne, white angels . . . I moved forward toward the lacy, supple Gothic arches, pinnacles and pillars, thinking, if this were music it would be trills played on the highest notes of violins." She felt as if she had climbed there "on Jacob's ladder, in a dream."

Hannah remained outside for almost an hour before she reluctantly came down. "It hurt so to leave the brilliance, the height, the peacefulness. I could take none of it with me." As she slowly descended, however, she realized that she was taking something with her, something she would keep forever—a memory, "an everlasting memory," she wrote, "of a great longing for light, for height, for peace."

The memory and the longing stayed with her through all the years to come, growing stronger and more urgent as the world became more cruel and more chaotic. Perhaps they explain why, for Hannah, the heights held no terror, and why it was fitting that she chose, when the time for choosing came, an act of resistance that began in the sky.

CHAPTER 3

1937-38

"Why is it necessary to ruin the world... when everything could be so pleasant?"

IN September 1937, when Hannah returned to school, she found that her Jewishness had become a continuing and public issue. At a meeting held the first week, she was proposed by her classmates for the job of Secretary of the Literary Society. Hannah was popular in her own class, having been together with the same girls for seven years. But the girls in the class ahead of her objected to her nomination because she was Jewish.

Hannah sat quietly through the entire meeting, "apparently calm and controlled," her mother wrote later. But she was deeply hurt. Later, her teacher condemned the students and urged Hannah to continue to work with the Society. But she would not hear of it. "The Literary Society generally accepts officers elected by the class, but in this case they called for a new election, and nominated two other girls to stand with me as candidates . . . . Had I not been elected I would not have said a word," Hannah wrote in her diary. "Now I don't want to take part in, or have anything to do with, the work of the Society, and don't care about it any more."

Her teacher later said that she had never seen anyone as "unjustly hurt" as Hannah had been. "I am very much afraid it will leave an ineradicable, lifelong impression on her," she told Catherine. "She is still at the head of the class, and seemingly everything is proceeding along the usual lines. However, it seems to me that she has become very detached, even alienated, from us."

Hannah didn't dwell on the incident, or note very much about it in her diary, but it is clear that her teacher was correct. Although she continued to do well in her studies, her enthusiasm seems to have dimmed. For the first time she recorded in her diary that "life at school is rather dull. I am not really working."

Hannah's excitement about school never returned, but before long, her high spirits did. Throughout the following fall and winter, she filled her time happily with outings, parties, and special projects of her own choosing. "Oh, how wonderful it was yesterday," she wrote one snowy Sunday in November 1937. "We had planned an excursion . . . with the usual crowd, but there was such a fabulous snowfall in the early morning that naturally I immediately thought of going skiing. I didn't know how the others would feel, whether I would find anyone to go with . . . when first János, then Peter telephoned, both suggesting that we go skiing. . . . We didn't get back until five . . . it was really marvelous!"

One of her special projects was the study of English, a language she particularly enjoyed. In addition to studying it in school, she began writing to an English pen pal and reading novels in English on her own—*The Good Earth* was a special favorite. Hannah also enrolled in the English course offered at a language institute after school. When George, already fluent in French, decided to learn English too, brother and sister tutored each other.

"He is teaching me French once a week, and I am teaching him English," Hannah recorded in her diary. She also recorded the ups and downs of her relationship with Peter. "He gave me to understand that he loves me," she had written in October. Then she added carefully: "I did not say I loved him because had I said it, it might well have been untrue. Anyway, I'm happy."

By January, Peter was all but forgotten, Hannah having found she was a "bit bored" with the relationship after all, and the names of other young men turn up on the diary pages that follow. There was George, who was a "wonderful dancer" and a "rather nice fellow," Danny, who told her he had worked hard in school only to please her, and Náday, "attractive" and "intelligent," someone to whom Hannah felt she could "really talk."

Party followed party, outing followed outing. Hannah's descriptions were jubilant. People were "wonderful," parties were "brilliant," evenings at home "delightful." The situation in school notwithstanding, Hannah, halfway between sixteen and seventeen, was pleased with herself and delighted with the world.

About a January Saturday night at home she wrote, "We read aloud the letters Daddy wrote Mama. They are such humorous, dear letters that it's a joy to read them."

She described a party given by a friend as "a large-scale, brilliant evening, the entire atmosphere delightful and gay." The hours flew by, Hannah reported, and she didn't get home until four in the morning.

But in March, Hannah's diary took on a new and anxious tone. German troops had moved into Austria. Hitler's National Socialist Party—the Nazis—had taken over the Austrian government. "These events have caused indescribable tension in Hungary," Hannah wrote. "In school, on the street, even at parties, it is the main topic of discussion."

Hitler had become Chancellor of Germany in 1933, appealing to the German people's dissatisfaction with their place in the world and their misery with the unemployment, hunger and inflation that stalked them at home. Hitler had given them answers and solutions, telling them what he himself believed—that

Nazi campaign poster from 1932 calling
on the Germans to throw off the forces that had kept them weak
and to vote for Hitler.

the German people were superior to all other people and that they had been grievously mistreated, first by the French, who had defeated them in the Napoleonic Wars and left them a shattered nation, and then by the powers that had defeated them in World War I. But the root cause of their downfall, Hitler told the German people, was the Jews. Evil, filthy and corrupt, the Jews had insinuated themselves into German life and were weakening the German people, destroying them from within.

Nazi poster, prior to Hitler's election. It says: "Free from misery! Free from the Jews! Vote National Socialist Party."

May 1939 special edition of Die Sturmer, a leading German newspaper. The headline reads "Ritual Murder." The picture is a reproduction of a medieval painting showing Jews murdering Christian children. The bottom line was a national slogan: "The Jews are our misfortune."

In identifying the Jews as an alien and evil people, Hitler was echoing ideas and attitudes that had existed in Europe since at least the fourth century, when Constantine the Great made Christianity the official religion of his empire. The Jews, ordered to convert to Christianity, had refused and were thereupon denied the rights of citizenship. They became outsiders and outcasts. The account in the Gospels that blamed the Jews for the crucifixion of Jesus helped Christians to see Jews as morally vicious and depraved. By the fifth century, church officials as well as uneducated peasants often believed that Jews were "agents of the devil," hated by God. In times of epidemic disease, they were said to cause people to sicken and die. In times of crop failure, they were said to cause plants to wither in the ground. They were often accused of heinous acts, such as murdering Christian children and using their blood to make matzoh, the unleavened bread eaten during the Jewish holiday of Passover. In the sixteenth century, Martin Luther, whom Hitler often quoted, warned Christians about the Jews' foul nature: "Know, Christian," he wrote, "that next to the devil, thou hast no enemy more cruel, more venomous and violent than the Jew." "By defending myself against the Jew," Hitler wrote, "I am fighting for the work of the Lord." "Whoever knows the Jew knows the devil," was a German saying.

Jew-hating was given pseudo-scientific credentials in the nineteenth century, when a new definition of race was introduced and promoted, primarily by the French Count Joseph Arthur de Gobineau in his *Essay on the Inequality of the Human Races* and the Englishman Houston Stewart Chamberlain (who became a German citizen) in his book *The Foundations of the Nineteenth Century.* According to the new ideas about race, which were received more enthusiastically by the Germans than by any other Europeans, Jews were not simply people who held certain religious views, or who had a common history or who shared beliefs and values. Jews were a separate race of people, the "Semitic" race, which was a morally and spiritually inferior race, suited only for slavery. Nordic people, on the other hand, of whom the

Germans were the best examples, were "Aryan," members of the "Teutonic race," the morally and spiritually superior "master race." These ideas were widely accepted among uneducated people and among those whose feelings of anti-Semitism they seemed to legitimize. Hitler used them from the beginning to explain what he saw as his mission and the mission of the German people. "The Jew is the anti-man," he wrote, "the creature of another God." Jews represented evil, while the members of the Teutonic race represented human perfection. The two had been locked in mortal combat since the beginning of time. "Two worlds face one another," Hitler wrote. "The men of God and the men of Satan!" Hitler called on the German people to take up the struggle against the Jews, the "poisoners and defilers" who had settled among them, and thus enable the pure Teutonic race to fulfill its destiny and become the masters of the world.

Many historians now believe that Hitler's obsession with the Jews was so great that it motivated his desire for conquest. He wanted to control all of Europe, and eventually the world, so that he could destroy the Jews. It is incontrovertible that the destruction of the Jews was more important to him than military conquest—he defied his generals and put his armies in jeopardy rather than allow Jews who could be killed to slip through his fingers. Political power was meaningless unless it included the power to kill Jews. "If the Jews survive the war," said Hans Frank, Hitler's handpicked governor of occupied Poland, "victory will be in vain." But in 1938, the threat Germany posed to the world was not understood in the bizarre terms of Hitler's devil-filled vision. It was understood in the conventional terms of political and military conquest. "What will happen to us," Hannah wondered, after the German takeover of Austria ("us" meaning the Hungarians, not the Jews), "in the shadow of an eastward-expanding nation of seventy million?"

For weeks after she asked herself that question, Hannah wrote nothing at all in her diary. It wasn't because she was unaware of or unconcerned about politics. But, like most people at the time,

Anti-Semitic children's board game called Jews Get Out, widely
distributed in Germany in the 1930s. Games, movies and even popular
songs encouraged children to scorn Jews and to accept anti-Semitism
as entirely proper.

adults as well as young people, she seems to have been quite overwhelmed by what was happening.

"I'm ashamed not to have written anything about today's depressed, tense, agitated world," she wrote at the beginning of April, breaking her silence. "But one talks and hears so much about events in Austria, and one is so nervous about the local situation, that by the time it comes to writing about things, one feels too depressed and discouraged."

Soon, however, it was impossible to ignore or try to ignore the changes occurring in the world. George's plans first brought the issues into the heart of the Senesh family. Due to graduate from high school in May 1938, George had planned to leave for Austria in the summer and to study at an Austrian university in the fall. Because of the Nazi takeover, that was now impossible, and Catherine was thinking of sending George to France. Hannah's heart ached to think of him going so far away. What would happen if war broke out? Would he be able to return? Would he be all right in France? She "could hardly bear" to think of saying goodbye to him in such circumstances.

The situation in Hungary itself was becoming ominous. An anti-Jewish "Bill for the More Effective Protection of Social and Economic Life" was introduced to Parliament in March 1938. It asked that a quota of twenty percent be placed on the number of Jews allowed to engage in certain professions and occupations, and it stated that "the expansion of the Jews is as detrimental to the nation as it is dangerous. We must take steps to defend ourselves against their propagation. Their relegation to the background is a national duty." The bill, which became known as the First Jewish Bill, was frightening not only because it singled Jews out as alien and bad, but also because it demonstrated that Hungary wished to be counted on Germany's side. The reasons, however, had as much to do with territory as anti-Semitism. Hungary wanted the lands near Austria that had been taken from it at the end of World War I. Germany, advancing in that direction, would soon be in control of those lands. The Hungarian government believed that if it allied itself with Germany, those lands would be returned to it. Nevertheless the results of its official anti-Semitic actions were just as terrible for the Jews as if hostility toward them had been the only motive.

"People are talking about it [the bill] everywhere," Hannah wrote in her diary at the end of April. "There has been, and continues to be, terrible tension about it. . . . Commerce, industry, the theatre, cafés—everything is at a standstill while this matter is under discussion in Parliament. I wonder how all this will end?"

Public shows of hostility against Jews, rudeness and name-calling on the streets, began to be commonplace. No one who was Jewish was safe from it—not even people like the Seneshes, assimilated and established though they were. Hannah herself was subject to a tirade from a man who had taken the seat beside hers on the train. "I immediately noticed he wanted to get acquainted," Hannah wrote, "so I got out my book, *The Moon and Sixpence* by Somerset Maugham—a wonderful novel which actually deserves a separate paragraph—and started reading." But the man drew her into conversation anyway, telling her that he was a Presbyterian theologian and asking her what school she attended. When he suggested that Hannah take some theology courses, and she told him she was Jewish, he became "very upset" and asked for her name. When she refused to tell him, he launched into an attack on the Jews, accusing them of being clannish and unenlightened and claiming that "Jews stubbornly withdrew from all possible social contact and integration."

Hannah took the charge in stride. "I assured him," she noted dryly, "that this was certainly not why I wouldn't tell him my name."

The man, quite upset, said he would "wait for me one day after school," but Hannah was not intimidated. She "asked him not to do that," and left the train compartment. He did not follow her and "thus the matter ended." She had not been physically harmed, but the incident highlighted for her the anger and bad feelings that were in the air.

George's graduation, which took place early in May, filled Hannah with turmoil. "It was only then that I realized what it means to have him leaving home," she wrote, "without knowing what will become of him, when he will be able to return. How awful it must be for Mother."

A farewell gathering at the local synagogue in honor of the new graduates was sad and cheerless, since everyone knew that these Jewish boys would soon be scattered and could "look forward only to an uncertain future." The speaker tried to make his message confident and encouraging, but even so it sounded "hopeless and resigned," Hannah noted. "One can hardly feel otherwise these days."

Once her school term was over, with George and Catherine

planning George's trip to France, Hannah left Budapest for an inn on the shore of Lake Balaton. She had been invited to spend the summer there as a guest of the Virags, who were the owners and family friends. Hannah had been very pleased with the invitation since she thought she might like to open an inn of her own someday and this would be a good chance to learn about management and finances. By the time she arrived, however, it was clear her concerns were elsewhere. Her visit was only one day old when a reprimand from Madame Virag provoked her to tears.

"I'm going home," she reported in her diary.

Madame Virag had scolded Hannah for swimming too far from the shore. Normally, Hannah would have accepted such a reprimand calmly, but not now. "I spoke politely," she wrote, "but felt near to breaking point and began crying, so ran to my room. I locked the door, and cried for a long time."

Madame Virag later came to Hannah's room to comfort her and to assure her that she did not want her to leave. "She asked me not to let the same thing happen again, kissed me, and entreated me to stop crying. Of course this is easier said than done," Hannah wrote. She managed to rally her spirits but there was no longer any denying the strain she was under.

Two weeks later George boarded his train for France. It made a routine stop near Lake Balaton, and Hannah went to the station to say goodbye. In what seems like an effort to avoid showing their feelings, brother and sister chatted about what Hannah called "banalities"—tennis rackets, Italian lessons, mutual friends, and the length of the swimming pool in Milan. But after the train pulled out and Hannah returned to the inn alone, she wrote a poem called "Farewell."*

> You left. We waved a long while.
> Porters clattered behind.
> We watched and you disappeared.

*Hannah used "we" and "our" where "I" and "my" might be used today, because at that time it wasn't considered proper to use first person singular pronouns.

Life took you. You were happy.
Maybe your heart had songs within.
Our tears were well hidden.

Wordless, we went home
Watching the sky, pale and blue,
And our soul, unseen and secretly
Is waving still to you.

Hannah's remaining days at the inn passed quietly. She loved the lake, especially in stormy weather, and she went swimming and boating daily. The night before she returned to Budapest, she celebrated her seventeenth birthday, surrounded by friends. "At midnight we drank to my health," she wrote of the cheerful occasion, "danced a bit, and at about two in the morning went home."

Still, she was happy to return home, and to be with her mother again. They decided to spend most of August at a small hotel in the mountain village of Biela-Voda where other family members would also be staying. It was expensive, but "everyone has now lost the value of money," Hannah noted, because they knew that what happened in Austria might soon happen in Hungary too. "If it does," Hannah wrote, "it will make really very little difference how much one has left for them to confiscate."

Before leaving for Biela-Voda, Hannah sought professional criticism for her poetry, having gotten to the point where she wanted something other than "the praise of family and close friends." She sent her work to Piroska Reichardt, a journalist who worked for the most highly respected literary magazine in Hungary at that time. Then, at Madame Reichardt's invitation, Hannah visited her in person.

"She received me by saying the poems surprised her," Hannah wrote happily, "and she thinks I'm talented."

Piroska pointed out some of the weaknesses of Hannah's work—the poems were apt to be too long, she thought, sometimes the form was neglected for the sake of the content, and

sometimes Hannah's manner of expression was "rather imma-
ture." But on the whole, she was very encouraging and Hannah
was greatly heartened.

Inspired by the critique, eager to work at writing, Hannah's
spirits were high as she left Budapest with her mother. She was
exhilarated, finding the setting "truly wonderful" and the company "absolutely delightful." Days of hiking through the mountains were followed by nights of singing around the fireplace,
walks under the stars—and Ping-Pong. The subject of politics
hardly entered her mind, and when it did, she experienced only
a simple rush of enthusiasm for her native land, the kind of
uncritical patriotism any young person might feel.

"Last night we went for a walk, and this morning I got up
at five and went for a walk again," she wrote soon after their
arrival. "It was marvelous. I was all alone, the air was heavenly,
the view superb. I saw the sunrise, sang, picked strawberries
. . . looked for a four-leaf clover . . . carved the map of Hungary
on a bench and the letters N.N.S. [which stood for 'No, No,
Never!' a popular slogan that meant that Hungary would never
give up the fight to regain the land it had lost in the First World
War], then sat on a tree stump and marveled at the view. Stupen-
dous!"

One night about one week into her stay, Hannah and her
cousin Evi performed a skit of their own creation. They called
it "The Proposal." They made costumes, constructed props and
acted out marriage proposals as they might have occurred in four
different eras: 1000 B.C.E., the time of the Crusades, the age of
their grandmothers, and the future. Afterward, there was a dance.
"Not that there is a single boy worth writing about," Hannah
noted wryly. "But all the girls are very nice."

Back in Budapest in the end of August, Hannah reluctantly
prepared for her last year of school, knowing that "unpleasant-
nesses" similar to the incident at the Literary Society were likely
to occur again. Arrow Cross, the organization of Hungarian
Nazis, was bigger than it had ever been, and it was growing.
Many Jewish families, including several close to the Seneshes,

were converting to Christianity, despite the fact that under the First Jewish Bill, which had become a law in May 1938, Jews who converted to Christianity after July 31, 1919, were still considered Jews, as were all people born to Jewish parents after July 31, 1919, regardless of their beliefs or practices. And as bad as things seemed to be in Hungary, Jews from Austria and Czechoslovakia as well as Germany were arriving by the thousands. These refugees talked about assault and murder of Jews in their homelands, of mass arrests, destruction of property, arson, terror, hunger and laws and regulations against Jews that made Hungary's laws seem almost negligible. The lovely days Hannah had spent in the mountains seemed to belong to another lifetime. "Why," Hannah wondered shortly after school began, "is it necessary to ruin the world . . . when everything could be so pleasant?"

CHAPTER 4
1938-39
"I am a Jew and am proud of it"

November 9, 1938: Teletype Message

To: All Police Precincts of the Reich
From: Gestapo Headquarters, Berlin

This teleprinter message is secret: at very short notice, actions against Jews, especially against their synagogues, will take place throughout the whole of Germany. They are not to be stopped.

AND they were not stopped. Between midnight and dawn of November 10, 1938, fires were started in every town and village in Germany. Three hundred synagogues were allowed to burn to the ground. Mobs surged through the streets of every German city. They were urged on by speeches and rallies organized by the government, and led by out-of-uniform Storm Troopers, the infamous SA men, as well as members of the SS (Schutzstaffel), the elite blackshirted "security" corps, who were

*Interior of Fasanenstrasse synagogue
in Berlin before and after
Kristallnacht.*

trained to think of themselves as superior even to other Germans. Seventy-five hundred shops, homes, offices and community buildings belonging to Jews were gutted. Damages were estimated at several hundred million marks. One hundred Jews were murdered on that night, and twenty-six thousand Jews arrested.

"Jewish dwellings were smashed into," reported the American Consul in Leipzig, David Buffum, "and the contents demolished or looted. In one of the Jewish sections, an eighteen-year-old boy was hurled from a three story window to land with both legs broken on a street littered with burning beds and other household furniture. . . . Jewish shop windows by the hundreds were systematically and wantonly smashed throughout the city. . . . The main streets were a positive litter of shattered plate glass. . . . The debacle was executed by SS men and Storm Troopers not in uniform, each group having been provided with hammers, axes, crowbars and incendiary bombs. . . ."

In Berlin, special squads isolated Jewish buildings, cut phone lines and switched off electric power. Police rerouted traffic away from the areas that were going to be attacked. One fourteen-year-old boy, who was with his mother as a crowd of men pushed their way through their apartment destroying everything they could, said: "We felt as though we had lost our minds."

In Frankfurt, the riots started at 5 A.M. when the main synagogue was set on fire. One hour later Jewish homes were broken into, their contents hacked and burned. Men, women and children were driven into the streets and herded together in the town's festival hall. One of the prisoners, a well-known opera singer, was made to sing an aria from *The Magic Flute:* "In this sacred grove which knows no hate." "There was much laughter," said a witness.

The things that were done on that night "would seem unreal to one living in an enlightened country during the twentieth century if one had not actually been a witness," wrote the American Consul in Stuttgart, Samuel Honaker. It was the first large-scale public show of Nazi power and intentions toward the Jews. It has come to be called Kristallnacht, the Night of Glass. And it was only the beginning.

Catherine remembers Hannah saying to her that fall that "even if she had not happened to be born a Jew she would still

Synagogue in Baden-Baden set on fire during Kristallnacht. Firefighters were ordered to protect surrounding buildings, if they were not owned by Jews, but to make sure the synagogues burned.

be on the side of the Jews because one must help, by all possible means, a people who were being treated so unjustly now, and who had been abused so miserably throughout history."

Catherine understood Hannah's feelings completely, but she did not think there was anything they could do to help. She believed they must wait out the storm of anti-Semitism sweeping through Europe. People would come to their senses sooner or later, she thought, and the storm would die down. In the meantime they must try to remain calm. Hannah, however, had come to a very different understanding of the situation and a very different vision of the future. She was now a Zionist.

"This word stands for a tremendous number of things," she wrote in her diary toward the end of October. "To me it means, in short, that I now consciously and strongly feel I am a Jew, and am proud of it. My primary aim is to go to Palestine, to work for it."

The main shopping street in Magdeburg after Kristallnacht.
Plate glass windows have been smashed and the street
is littered with debris.

Zionism had been a small, slowly growing movement among the Jews of Europe for over fifty years. Hannah had not agreed with its ideas when she first heard them. But now she believed, as Zionists did, that the Jews of Europe had reached a dead end, that the future held nothing but more humiliation for them, and that they ought to leave. There was no solution to the problem of anti-Semitism in Europe. There was nothing the Jews could do to end it, because it wasn't anything they did that caused it. It was what they were in the eyes of others: strangers, outsiders, people who did not belong.

"In Europe, the Jew is neither friend nor foe, but an alien," wrote Moshe Leib Lilienblum, a Russian Jew and one of the first Zionist thinkers. "We may not think of ourselves as strangers," he wrote, "but others do. And though strangers may sometimes be received as guests, they must not compete with members of the household. Thus the spectacle of a Jew who has eaten remains intolerable to the non-Jew who is hungry. There is nothing we can do to avoid the conflict."

Even in the best of times, Jews had been prevented by law from owning land and holding certain jobs. They had been made to live in certain restricted zones and towns to discourage them from mingling with other people. In the worst of times, they had been used as scapegoats, brutalized, vandalized and murdered, made to leave their homes, expelled from town, state and kingdom, blamed for whatever was wrong with the world, accused of the most horrible crimes.

"For more than 600 years we have been proving to Europe in vain that we neither eat human flesh nor drink Christian blood," Lilienblum wrote in 1882. "What disgrace! What shame!"

If the Jews could not change the world, Lilienblum said, or wait for it to change, they could and must change themselves. If they would always be strangers in Europe, they must leave Europe. If they had no place to go, they must make a place.

"All strangers have a home somewhere," Lilienblum wrote, "except the Jews." He urged them to return to the land of their origin, the Holy Land of the Bible, which in their hearts and prayers had never been forgotten. The idea of someday returning to Israel had lost its practical aspect over the centuries—"someday" coming to mean "not now" and "not in our lifetime"—but it had never been abandoned.

"Why should we be strangers in foreign lands," Lilienblum wrote now, "when the land of our forefathers is not yet forgotten on the face of the earth. It is still desolate and capable of receiving our people. We must purchase much land and many estates and slowly settle there."

At the time of Lilienblum's writing, the biblical Holy Lands were part of what was called Palestine, a thinly populated area on the shore of the Mediterranean Sea. It was without industry, farmable land, railroads or roads. It was not an independent state but a territory belonging to Turkey. A small number of Jews had always lived in what they called "the Land" (*Eretz*), or "the Land of Israel" (*Eretz Israel*), by which they meant not a civil or political state but the place of their historic and religious origin. Most of them lived in the four "holy cities" of Jerusalem, Safed, Tiberias and Hebron. Highly religious and inclined toward mysticism, they felt that in the land of the Bible they were closest to God. Now Lilienblum urged all Jews to look toward Palestine, not for religious reasons, but because without a homeland of their own they would always be in danger. Their experience in Europe had proven that with complete clarity.

"The idea of rescue was always the ultimate urge behind the Zionist movement," explained Israeli writer Amos Elon. "Beyond all other considerations, the desire to save Jews from total dependence upon others . . . to save them from being at the mercy of others, was Zionism's deepest, most fundamental rationale."

Lilienblum developed his ideas in the 1880s, as a wave of pogroms—attacks upon Jews and Jewish villages—swept across the Russian Pale of Settlement, the only area in Russia in which Jews were allowed to live. A few years earlier, there had been hope that the Jews of Russia, like the Jews of Western Europe, might be emancipated someday. But that hope was abandoned when the pogroms began. Police and government troops joined the attacking peasants as they swooped down on Jewish villages, raiding, murdering, stealing, setting fires and destroying property at will. The Russian government, a monarchy, was the most backward and corrupt in Europe. It encouraged pogroms because it hoped they would serve as outlets for the anger of the poor and increasingly rebellious peasants, distractions from their real problems. The Jews, unarmed and outnumbered, disliked and distrusted, made easy targets and perfect scapegoats.

Lilienblum remembered how he himself had hidden in the cellar of his house while rioters rampaged through the streets outside. "The women shrieked and wailed, hugging their children to their breasts, and did not know where to turn," he wrote in his diary. "The men stood by dumbfounded."

The Jews "flee like mice, hide like beetles, and die like dogs wherever they be found," wrote Nahum Bialik, the great poet of the Russian Jews and of the Zionist movement. The poem was called "In the City of Slaughter."

With the pogroms, Russia became a country to be abandoned. When they began, over 6,000,000 Jews were living there —seventy percent of all the Jews in Europe, and over half of all the Jews in the world. First by the hundreds, then by the thousands, and then by the hundreds of thousands, they made their way to the Russian borders in what is sometimes called the "second exodus." A handful headed for Palestine, but the great majority headed for the emancipated states of Western Europe and for America. They believed, as did most Jews in the West, that emancipation had launched a new era in Western Europe and that anti-Semitism was or soon would be a thing of the past. By the end of the nineteenth century, however, it had become clear that this was not true. Emancipation had not brought an end to anti-Semitism, not even in what seemed to be the most liberal and sophisticated communities. If proof was needed, proof was found in the infamous case of Alfred Dreyfus, the Jewish French Army officer wrongly accused and unjustly convicted of treason.

"What made me into a Zionist was the Dreyfus case," said Theodore Herzl, often called the founder of modern Zionism. Herzl was a successful Viennese journalist, an educated assimilated Jew who had been only marginally concerned with anti-Semitism until he experienced the depth and strength of it for himself in 1894 while covering the trial of Alfred Dreyfus in Paris. Dreyfus was eventually exonerated. But the charges—that he had passed military secrets to the Germans—and the trial that followed, unleashed a fury of anti-Semitic feeling that was so unexpected and so bitter that Jews throughout Europe were stunned. Anti-Semitism was not on the wane; it had just been underground. The trial of a Jew for treason brought it into the open. Many Jews reasoned that if such feelings existed among the non-Jews of France—the cultural center of Europe and the most civilized state of all, the land that had produced the revolutionary Declaration of the Rights of Man and led Europe in celebrating "liberty, equality, fraternity" for all human beings—then anti-Semitism was so deeply entrenched it might never be fully understood or fully eradicated from the European mind. Herzl was in the crowd that gathered to watch Dreyfus be stripped of his military rank and placed in chains. He saw firsthand as French citizens spat at the bewildered young officer and screamed, "Death to the Jews!" "We are one people," Herzl wrote afterward. "Our enemies have made us one."

Under Herzl's leadership, Zionism became a political movement. He devoted himself to it entirely, consulting with the sultan of Turkey, the emperor of Germany, the king of Italy and leaders of the British government in an attempt to gain political acceptance for the idea of a Jewish nation and a legal basis for its creation. Although at Herzl's death in 1904, a Jewish state had not yet come into being, the seeds had been planted and the political groundwork laid.

In the decade following his death, more and more Jews from both Eastern and Western Europe began making their way to Palestine. More land was purchased, settlements were built, acreage that had been barren for centuries was reclaimed for farming. In 1917, Great Britain announced in the Balfour Declaration that it viewed "with favor" the establishment of a Jewish homeland in Palestine. After World War I, the League of Nations—created to help nations resolve problems peacefully—gave control of the 60,000 square miles comprising the Palestinian territory to the British, with the understanding that they would "help to facilitate" the creation of such a homeland there "under suitable conditions." Immigration doubled and then tripled. By the 1930s, with the rise of Hitler, the Zionist answer seemed to even greater numbers of Jews to be the only answer to the torment their lives in Europe had become.

"I am determinedly and purposefully preparing for life in Palestine," Hannah wrote in her diary in November 1938. She wanted to go at the end of the school year, as soon as she graduated from high school. "Although I confess that in many respects it's painful to tear myself from my Hungarian sentiments, I must do so in my own interest," she wrote, "and the interests of Jewry. Our two-thousand-year history justifies us, the present compels us, the future gives us confidence. Whoever is aware of his Jewishness cannot continue with his eyes shut."

A month and a half later, on December 23, 1938, the Second Jewish Bill was turned into law by the Hungarian Parliament. It was entitled "A Bill to Restrict Jewish Penetration in the Public Affairs and the Economic Life of the Country." It prohibited Jews from holding leading positions in the communications media, barred them from entering the professions until such time as they fell to below six percent of the total, and authorized the government to take, with compensation, all land owned by Jews anywhere in the country. It also defined exactly who was and who was not to be considered a Jew—a necessity in light of the fact that most Hungarian Jews were well assimilated and there had been many intermarriages, children of intermarriages and outright conversions. According to this new law a Jew was not only anyone who currently practiced the Jewish religion, but also anyone who had been a Jew and had converted to Christianity: (1) on or after their seventh birthday; (2) before their seventh birthday, but whose parent or parents had not converted by January 1, 1939; (3) before their seventh birthday, and whose parents had converted by January 1, 1939, but whose family had come to Hungary after 1849. This definition was even stricter and more inclusive than the definition in Hitler's Germany. According to the German definition, a Jew was: (1) anyone with three or more Jewish grandparents; (2) anyone with two Jewish grandparents who practiced the Jewish religion on September 15, 1935, or later; (3) anyone who was married to a person defined as a Jew on September 15, 1935, or later; (4) anyone who was the child of a Jewish mother.

Jews throughout Hungary had struggled for the defeat of this bill. They called upon the government to stand by the principles of equality in the Hungarian constitution. But the bill had passed easily into law, hailed by pro-Nazi officials in the government as "the most beautiful Christmas present we could ever have hoped for."

Noting that the bill did not address the real problems facing Hungary, but simply made scapegoats of the Jews, Hannah was dismayed but not surprised. "Of course," she wrote, "this was to be expected."

She had begun to study Hebrew—"in it is the spirit of our people," she wrote—and had joined a Zionist discussion group, where she was greatly inspired by a woman who had actually been to Palestine and been "enchanted" by it.

"She . . . told me all sorts of wonderful things about the Land," Hannah wrote. "Listening to her was a joy. Everything that is beautiful, cheerful, and of some consolation to the Jews stems from Palestine."

Hannah's mother was dismayed. Like most of the people in her social circle, she believed that Hungarian Jews were safe, that they had a future in Hungary and that there was no reason for anyone to emigrate. More than that, she did not want to lose her daughter. George was already gone. She did not want Hannah to leave Hungary too.

But Hannah was committed. She had found a new center for her life in Zionism. It gave her a way of understanding the world, an ideal that inspired her and a purpose to which she wished to devote herself entirely.

"One needs something to believe in," she wrote in her diary, "something for which one can have wholehearted enthusiasm. One needs to feel that one's life has meaning, that one is needed in this world. Zionism fulfills all this for me. . . . I now feel firm ground under my feet, and can see a definite goal toward which it is really worth striving. . . . I've become a different person, and it's a very good feeling."

Catherine raised every objection she could think of, but Hannah had an answer for them all. "When I asked her what had become of her ambition to be a professional writer," Catherine wrote, "she answered, 'That question is dwarfed by present burning problems.' "

Nevertheless, Hannah understood Catherine's feelings and to an extent, she even shared them. "I would be so happy if Mother came [to Palestine] too," she wrote in her diary. "The three of us must not be torn apart, must not go three different ways."

Even so, she did not doubt the need to emigrate or the rightness of her doing so. She was convinced that anti-Semitism was "an illness which can neither be fought against with words, nor cured with superficial treatment." It would only be cured, she believed, when there was a Jewish nation, a "Homeland for the Jewish spirit and the Jewish people." And she wanted, more than anything else, to help in its creation. "I don't want to work only for myself and in my own interests," she wrote, "but for the mutual good of Jewish aims."

Years later, Catherine recalled how she had tried to remain firm in her opposition to Hannah's plans. But finally Hannah "tackled" her with this statement: "Mother," she said, "if you don't agree to my going, of course I won't go. But I want you to know I feel miserable in this environment, and don't wish to live in it."

At this, in the late winter of 1938–39, Catherine conceded, and Hannah was filled with love and gratitude. Her involvement with Zionism was so deep that there seemed to be no room in her feelings for anything else.

"Perhaps I don't exaggerate," she noted in her diary on March 10, 1939, "if I write that the only thing I'm committed to, in which I believe, is Zionism. . . . I can barely think of anything else. I am not afraid of being one-sided. Until now I have had to cast my sights in many directions. Now I have the right to look only in one direction—the direction of Jewry, Palestine and our future."

The life she had lived just the year before, and that most of her friends were still living, no longer made any sense to her at all. The goals she had had no longer seemed important. School had become a burden. A career as a writer seemed a luxury that she as a Jew could not afford. The occasion of her "coming out" party, her official social debut, would normally have been the most important event of her life, but now it seemed instead "frivolous" and "empty." The celebration left her feeling restless, lonely and more eager than ever to move on.

"I kept thinking how nice it would have been to have put all the money the party cost into the collection box of the Keren Kayemet [the Jewish National Fund]," she wrote the next day. "Oh, dear, I would like best of all to go to Palestine now. I would be glad to forfeit my graduation, everything. . . . I just can't live here any longer, can't stand my old group of friends, studying, or any of the things with which I've been familiar up till now. . . . A ship is leaving today with a great many Hungarian Jews aboard. I so wish I could have gone with them."

"Though she was physically still with me," her mother wrote of Hannah, "she was actually already living in another world. Outwardly she appeared controlled, as always, but anyone close to her could sense the excitement and stirrings within her."

In March 1939, Hannah applied for admission to the agricultural school in Nahalal, Palestine. Her mother was very distressed. If Hannah had to go to Palestine, she said, why not attend the University of Jerusalem. There, "according to her talents and capabilities," she really belonged, and there she would certainly prove more useful and productive than in something so "completely alien to her as farm work." But Hannah didn't want simply to live in Palestine. She wanted to be a pioneer, to work on the land, to build a nation that could feed itself, for the Jewish people who would come after her.

"There are already far too many intellectuals in Palestine," she said to her mother. "The great need is for workers who can help build the country. Who can do the work if not we, the youth?"

Hannah wrote her application to the agricultural school entirely in Hebrew. "May I request a favorable decision?" she wrote in the last paragraph. "An acceptance to the school would give me great joy and happiness. It would be the first step toward the realization of my life's ambition."

The next month, during the Easter holiday, Hannah and Catherine traveled to France to visit George. To Hannah's immense pleasure, she found that he too had become a Zionist. Catherine listened to her children discuss their plans with a sense of loneliness and foreboding.

"They discussed and planned the future with profound, youthful zeal, eyes sparkling," she wrote later. "They decided Hannah would emigrate within a few months, and that George would follow when his studies were completed. Their great concern was for me to join them. Would we ever again sit together like this, I wondered, the three of us?"

Early that summer, Hannah graduated school *summa cum laude,* "with high honors." By that time, the fact that she was planning to emigrate was common knowledge, and several of Hannah's teachers approached Catherine privately. They urged her to persuade her daughter not to go, for she was a young woman of real talent and would do brilliantly at the university.

Although the number of Jews allowed to attend the university had been officially restricted by the Second Jewish Bill, they assured Catherine that with their influence, Hannah was guaranteed a place. Hannah found their assurances almost insulting.

Hannah's high school graduation picture, June 20, 1939.

"Perhaps I ought to be impressed that in view of graduating *summa cum laude,* and with a plethora of recommendations from teachers and friends, I can get into the university, while a Gentile who just barely squeezed through the exams can sail in!" she scoffed. "Besides, are they really incapable of understanding that I don't want to be just a student, that I have plans, dreams, ambitions, and that the road to their fulfillment would only be barred to me here?"

In July, Hannah and Catherine went to an inn in the country, where Hannah studied Hebrew in the morning and worked in the garden in the afternoon to prepare herself for the work she would do in Palestine. Her Certificate of Immigration was due to arrive soon. It was the last thing she needed before she could plan her journey out of Hungary. As she waited, she was filled with a sense of well-being.

"I know these are the most beautiful years of my life," she wrote on her eighteenth birthday, July 17, 1939. "I am happy with my life, with everything that surrounds me. I believe in the future. My ideal fills my entire being." Her diary was now written exclusively in Hebrew. "Though I write less than if I were writing in Hungarian," she explained, "I do better thinking a little bit in Hebrew than a lot in Hungarian."

Four days later, the certificate arrived.

"I've got it, I've got it!" she wrote in great excitement. "I read and re-read the letter bearing the good news, now I can't find words to express what I feel. I have no feeling other than overwhelming happiness."

Catherine was subdued, and Hannah understood.

"She is filled with conflicting emotions," she wrote about her mother, "and is really very brave. I won't ever forget her sacrifice. Not many mothers would behave as she is behaving."

Nevertheless, Hannah's joy was intense.

"I have to be in Palestine by the end of September," she wrote. "I won't write any more now, but there is one more thing I would like to say to everyone, to all those who helped me, to God, to my mother: Thank you!"

Soon after, Hannah and Catherine returned to Budapest and Hannah began to make final preparations for her departure. Rosika, the Senesh housekeeper for many years, worked with her, for Catherine could not bring herself to help. One day, Hannah was going excitedly from train line to ticket agent when she was stricken with a mild but continuous pain in her chest. Because her father had died of heart failure, Hannah was very frightened.

"It's so dreadful," she wrote in her diary. "I still haven't been to see a doctor, I still haven't told my mother, and I don't want to believe it yet. I pray it's not true, that it will pass."

If her heart was not well, Hannah realized, she would not be able to do the work required of her at the agricultural school. They would consider her irresponsible for even going there. But if she gave up her place, and did not go where she "most longed to go," she might never have the chance again.

"What shall I do?" she wrote. "I can't discuss this with Mother. I must decide alone. . . . My God, my God, let this be just a bad dream."

A week after that entry, when the pain still had not gone away, Hannah went to the family doctor and told him everything. He examined her and found that there was nothing wrong with her heart: the pain was merely caused by nervous tension.

On the first day of September, Germany invaded Poland. On the second, Great Britain came to the aid of Poland, its ally, and declared war on Germany. The following day, France joined Great Britain. World War II had begun. All routes for civilian travel out of Hungary were sealed. Hannah was beside herself.

"I resigned myself to this new situation," her mother wrote, "but not she."

Hannah went to the office of the Representative of Palestine, the office of the Jewish Social Aid agency, wherever she thought there might be someone who could help her obtain passage out of Hungary. Finally, on the day before Rosh Hashanah, the Jewish New Year, a solemn day that marks the birthday of the world, and that begins a ten-day period of reflection on one's life, repentance for one's sins and meditation about God and righteousness, Hannah located a group of Slovaks en route to Palestine who could include her in their number. After begging Catherine to go with her, Hannah hurried with her mother to the Jewish Social Aid office to arrange her papers. An official there recognized "the daughter of Bela Senesh" and pushed Hannah's papers through. Her train would leave at noon the next day.

"I felt," Catherine wrote later, "as though ice were flowing through my veins."

She and Hannah packed all night. Their closest relatives and a few good friends came to say goodbye. At one o'clock the next day, September 13, 1939, they left the house together.

"We both tried to control our emotions," Catherine wrote. "But at the last moment, as she put her arms around our faithful Rosika, Hannah began sobbing and said, 'Rosi, take care of Mama.'"

On the train, Hannah stood at the window, hardly able to choke back her sobs. As the train pulled out, it seemed to Catherine that a cloud had fallen over the entire station. When she arrived home it was dusk.

"The melancholy mood of Rosh Hashanah had already settled over the empty house," she wrote years later, "and the flickering candles seemed to magnify my feelings. Fate had relentlessly intruded upon our lives, torn our little family apart, scattered us in three directions."

CHAPTER 5

1939-40

"Send me to serve the beautiful and the good"

ROSH HASHANAH, the turn of the year, is followed ten days later by Yom Kippur, the Day of Atonement. On that day, the period of repentance ends. The Book of Life and the Book of Death, in which God had written on Rosh Hashanah, and which had remained open throughout the period of repentance, are closed. The fate of every living creature is sealed for the coming year. On Yom Kippur in 1939, Hannah had been in Palestine for four days.

"A little *Sabra* * is climbing up the olive tree directly behind me," she wrote in her diary on that Yom Kippur day, September 23, 1939. "In front of me are cypress trees, cacti, the Emek Valley. I am in Nahalal, in Eretz. I am home."

The journey from Hungary had taken almost seven days, two by train and five aboard the Rumanian ship *Bessarabia*. Hannah had found it all exciting, especially the sea journey. She had asked

---

Sabra, a kind of cactus. Its fruit is thorny outside but sweet inside. The "Sabras," Israeli-born children, are supposed to be rough (outside) but good (inside).

Hannah's first day in Palestine (September, 1939).

for and gotten an upper berth, right next to the porthole where it was "nice and airy." She slept well every night, rose happily with the dawn every morning, roamed the ship from stem to stern and practiced Hebrew with the Palestinians, French with the Poles.

In "the magnificent harbor of Haifa," where the ship finally docked, Hannah was met by an official who helped her arrange the bus trip to Nahalal itself. As she rode through the northern Emek, Hannah marveled at the landscape, the "flocks of straggling sheep . . . huge cacti and beautiful fruit orchards." Her excitement was almost more than she could contain. And although she felt anxious and lonely on the night before Yom Kippur (confiding to her diary that she had wept, that it had felt good to "let go, to cry for once"), she quickly recovered her spirit and her confidence. "Even behind the tears I felt I had done the right thing," she wrote. "This is where my life's ambition . . . binds me."

For several weeks after her arrival in Nahalal, Hannah was so taken up with her new routine—six hours a day of practical work and three hours of classroom work—that she couldn't focus on what she called "personal matters" at all. "The bell rings at

Unloading seedlings at Nahalal Agricultural Training School for Girls.

Students at work in the nursery at Nahalal.

5:30 A.M.," she wrote her mother. "My two roommates begin to stir and I get up as well. We have a wash basin in our room, so I can brush my teeth comfortably, get washed, dress. . . . At six the bell rings again: we have to go to class. So far we've had classes in four subjects: chemistry, botany, general agriculture and fruit gardening. . . . We're about to have our first class in dairy farming, and nutrition is also included in the curriculum. Of course, there's also Hebrew class—and that's all so far."

The first class ended at seven, and was followed by a breakfast of tea, tomatoes, butter, cheese and bread. Then it was out to the fruit orchard, where the work varied with the day and season. Hannah's first assignment was picking olives, work she found easy but boring. Her next assignment was in the vineyard, where she hoed around the roots and tied back the branches. "Believe me," her letter to Catherine said, "it's a wonderful feeling to look at a completed row of vines, and the work isn't even hard."

At noon the girls returned to their rooms, washed up and headed for the dining hall where, Hannah wrote, "with a hearty appetite—and as far as I'm concerned in the best possible humor . . . we sit down to eat."

The food was unusual for Hannah and most of the time she

didn't know what it was called. "All I know about the food," she wrote, "is that I eat it and like it. Exactly what it is, its ingredients, I really don't know."

The girls finished lunch at twelve-thirty and at one-thirty began their afternoon work. At three they "rushed" in for tea, and at three-thirty, classes began again. From four-thirty to six-thirty they were free, and at six-thirty they went to their last class.

"On the whole," Hannah wrote, "I understand the lessons quite well. I take notes, particularly of new words, and thus things progress. At seven-thirty, supper, which is also good and varied. Afterward news on the radio which I don't often listen to because as yet I don't understand it very well. Only what they say about France and Hungary really interests me, and the local news, of course. Heaven knows Europe is very far from here."

In her willingness to turn her back on Europe, and her passion to build, through her own labor, a new country, Hannah was one with the other Zionists of Europe who had left old jobs and social roles behind and who had joyously acquired the physical skills of survival and self-reliance in Palestine. In Europe they had been students, shopkeepers, lawyers, teachers, scholars. In Palestine they became farmers, shepherds, carpenters. They believed in labor and in the new country they were building with their own hands.

The kibbutz—a community of farmer-settlers who own their land in common, make decisions democratically, share the work and the products of work—was a social structure created by the Zionists from Europe. It suited their practical needs, for only by working together could they build productive farms and secure settlements. And it fulfilled their vision of a just community, in which people would be cooperative rather than competitive, where each individual would be treated with respect, and where everyone would work for the good of all.

Zionists like Hannah called themselves not *menagirim,* the Hebrew word for "immigrant," but *olim,* which means "those who ascend." They called the wave of migration of which they

were a part *ha aliyah,* "the going up," because for them, the move
to Palestine was both a physical move and a spiritual one, a means
of spiritual rebirth. They believed that through their labor, they
would create a homeland for the Jewish people and they would
find their own souls. "We have come to the land to build and to be
rebuilt by it," was the refrain of a song every pioneer knew.
Hannah shared this belief although there were times, especially in
the beginning, when her hold on it wavered. She didn't write
about her feelings to her mother, toward whom she was always
reassuring, but she wrote about them in her letters to her brother
George.

"When one leaves work with a rake or a spade over one's
shoulder and looks at the Emek, the country's most fertile, beautiful area . . . it's a wonderful, wonderful feeling," she wrote in
her first letter to him. "But I want to be honest. This work doesn't
have just a romantic side. When I hoe, or clean something, or
wash dishes, or scatter the manure, I must confess the thought
strikes me . . . that I could be doing something better."

As surprising to Hannah as the boredom was the loneliness
she felt away from her family. About this, too, George was her
confidante.

"I think of you so much," she wrote in November 1939. "It
would be wonderful to sit down for a bit—or for a very long
while—and talk. Among the many things we would talk about
and discuss would be the things it is so difficult to write about
—not only because there are no words for such things, but
because one is so stupidly shy that one is ashamed to write about
one's feelings, even to those who are closest and dearest. For
instance, I am ashamed to write to you that here, beside the
typewriter, I've been crying. Though I could not tell you why,
because I like being here and am fine, and not disappointed in
anything. But I think you'll understand how it is just the same,
and that what I really miss is you and Mother."

Despite these low moments Hannah's spirits were often jubilant. In one of her roommates, a girl named Miryam, she found
a "best friend." Miryam had come to Nahalal at the same time

as Hannah, and had "similar goals" and "similar ideas." Sometimes the similarities between them created tension and competition. "We had many heated arguments," Hannah wrote in her diary. "There were times when our wrangling ended abruptly and in anger, as one or the other would say, 'I don't want to discuss this with you any further,' or would suddenly end the argument in mid-sentence with, 'That's enough! I want to sleep!' These heated discussions generally took place at night, after ten o'clock, and more than once were so stormy that our neighbors yelled, 'Stop it!' "

They were both "too tense," Hannah wrote, "too avid for everything in the Land." But they both "desperately wanted a new life," and found their visions reflected in each other.

"What is most important," Hannah wrote, "is that I was able to turn to her with all my problems. . . . I knew she understood me. . . . I always valued her opinions. . . . We also glanced at the world together, laughed together at its expense. . . . It took but a glance, a single word, or even just a hint, and we understood each other."

In January 1940, Hannah was assigned to work in the dairy barn, washing down the cows. The thought of her old schoolmates and how they would "turn up their noses" at such work made her smile. Indeed, there were many things about this assignment that Hannah found humorous. "If at times a cow, regardless of my nudging and pushing, refuses to stand up or lift a leg, or is reluctant to fulfill any other of my wishes," she wrote to her mother, "I take advantage of the opportunity to speak Hungarian, a language not often understood in this area, and wish the cow that which in Hebrew I don't know any way because as yet I haven't learned to swear in the language! But fortunately the cows don't understand either, and thus the relationship between us is most peaceful."

She enclosed a wild flower with her letter to Catherine to show her mother that in Palestine it was already spring. Also, the anniversary of her father's death was approaching, a day on which

Hannah would ordinarily have placed a flower on his grave. "I'll be thinking of you, dearest Mother, even more than usual, if that's possible."

Nine days after Hannah penned this letter, one of the founders of Nahalal died. The entire student body attended her funeral, and Hannah wrote about it to her mother. "Standing there among the graves I thought that a year ago, on almost precisely the same date, I had stood beside Daddy's grave, and perhaps at just that moment you were at the cemetery again, Mother dear, and it was so sad to think neither George nor I could be with you at such a time."

Hannah's love for her mother and the connection she felt to her did not lessen as the months passed. Her letters bear witness to both. "Distant . . . far away," Hannah wrote at the end of February. "One can no longer use old words. . . . Perhaps the distance is great in miles . . . but if I look at myself in the mirror and see my tangled hair I can actually feel your disapproving gaze upon me. If I meet someone for the first time the thought flashes through my mind, What would Mother think of him? If I do something I know is right, I know you, too, would approve, and I feel that our thoughts are meeting somewhere, perhaps midway, above the sea. I feel how strong and resilient is this unseen thread that binds us." She ended her letter with a "fervent request to heaven: Let the time come as quickly as possible when we will again be together."

During Hannah's first spring in Palestine, the spring of 1940, opposition to British rule there grew more and more bitter. Great Britain had not met the conditions spelled out by the League of Nations. Instead, from the beginning, it had considered Palestine not a place in which to help the Jews build a nation, but a link in the chain of the British Empire—an overland bridge to India —and a base of operations for the military defense of the Suez Canal. It had restricted Jewish settlers to 2,000 square miles of the 60,000 square miles it governed, and even that was done grudgingly. The Colonial Office, which planned policy for Palestine, sought to please the Arab nations surrounding Palestine as well as the Arab leaders in Palestine itself (even though some of them, like the Mufti of Jerusalem, were adventurers and opportunists rather than true leaders of their people). Their support, Great Britain believed, would be crucial if its imperial interests in the Middle East were ever threatened.

Objections poured in to the Colonial Office from the League of Nations, the United States government and members of the British Parliament itself. But British policy in Palestine continued to serve the interests of the British Empire. It was not designed to help, and it did not help the Jewish settlers live in peace with the Arabs and build a homeland in a portion of the vast territory. Resentment of British policies and personnel, who were often openly hostile toward the Jewish settlers, had been growing in Palestine throughout the 1930s. Then, in May 1939, the British had taken a step that was intolerable to the Jews there. In a document known as the White Paper, it announced its intention to end Jewish immigration to Palestine entirely. A maximum of 75,000 Jews would be allowed to enter over the next five years—10,000 a year and an additional 25,000 "as a contribution toward the solution of the Jewish refugee problem." After that, none.

The White Paper was denounced by non-Jews as well as Jews around the world. But it went into effect immediately, implemented by patrol boats, destroyers and later the Royal Air Force, which searched the sea for refugee boats. The first seizure occurred on June 1, when the Rumanian ship *Lizel* was caught off the coast of Palestine and its passengers, 900 Jews from Czechoslovakia and Austria, arrested and interned in British prison camps. On June 7, another ship was spotted in the waters around Haifa, its passengers arrested and imprisoned. On June 30, the ship *Astir* was seized with 724 passengers aboard, most of them refugees from the Polish city of Danzig. It was turned back to sea. Like most of the other refugee ships, the *Astir*'s voyage had been organized by a group called Mossad (Committee for Illegal Immigration), which had been created by Palestinian Jews as a lifeline to the Jews of Europe. Mossad agents had been at work

Illegal immigrants stealing ashore. Palestine, 1939-1940.

in almost every major European city since 1937, bribing, persuading, forging documents, hiring ships, trying to help people leave a hate-filled continent. Ironically, some of their most bitter confrontations were not with European governments, but with the British authorities in Palestine. On September 2, 1939, for example, the day after the German invasion of Poland, a ship called the *Tiger Hill* reached Palestine. The largest ship ever organized

British soldiers overpower an illegal immigrant, a former partisan, who was flushed out of his ship by tear gas.

by Mossad, the *Tiger Hill* was carrying 1,500 Polish Jews when British destroyers fired at it, the first shots fired by Britain after its declaration of war on Germany. Four passengers were killed, three women and one man.

British soldiers guard refugees who were arrested as they attempted to disembark near Haifa.

Throughout the fall and winter, Jewish sentiment toward Britain grew more and more bitter. The Irgun, a terrorist group, urged armed resistance with the aim of expelling the British from

Captured illegal immigrants in a holding cell in Haifa
awaiting deportation.

Palestine entirely. By the spring of 1940, the Land seemed ready
to explode.

"War against the British rule—it seems that is the desperate,
bitter public opinion," Hannah wrote in her diary in March of
that year. She thought such a war would be fruitless, a "meaningless waste of blood and life," and she tried to believe that it was
unnecessary, that the suffering of the Jewish people would not
continue. "It would be so good and so simple if with a prayer
such as, 'My Lord, help Your people . . . our people,' one could
trust and believe, and not pry into, or dwell upon, the possibilities
of the future," she wrote. But she could not "trust and believe,"
no matter how much she wished to, and she began to feel that
she was floundering. Her common sense told her that "war
against the British" would be futile. But how could common

sense be trusted in a world where so many people seemed to have lost their sense entirely?

"Who can answer these questions?" she wondered in her diary. "I feel very much alone. Sometimes I feel as if I am thinking of important things in a dream, making decisions about my life, and not understanding what it is all about."

Jews of Tel Aviv demonstrate against British rule because of the White Paper.

She continued to have faith in her work, however, and in fact to see it in more urgent terms than ever before. A desire to protect those who were helpless began to take shape more clearly in her thoughts. In botany class she learned about *calyptra,* the tough root cells that cushion and protect the plant's roots when they first penetrate the soil. As soon as the root is established, the calyptra atrophy and die. Hannah's teacher said they could be considered "the pioneers of the plants." His words seemed to fly "over the heads of the other pupils," Hannah noted. But they touched her heart.

"Here, in Nahalal," she wrote, "if one examines the lined faces of the farmers—who are young in years—one can't help but be struck by the strong imprint left by their battle with the soil. . . . They were the cells that perished so they could penetrate the soil and help to create roots for every plant. Shall our generation become such root cells too?" she wondered.

Scrubbing floors, studying nutrition, tying back the vines in the vineyard, she saw metaphors for the history of the Jewish people and found symbols for their struggles. Sorting grapefruit, putting the firm ones on the bottom and placing the battered ones on top, she thought that perhaps that was the way God had "arranged" the Jews. Perhaps "He piled the strong at the bottom," she wrote, "so they could bear the pressure which represented the weight of a developing country, while the battered remain for the top."

During this time Hannah was not always so serious or solemn. One Saturday—a day off for the students at Nahalal—she decided to hitchhike to Haifa. Her roommate Miryam could not go, so Hannah made her way to the junction alone. Several other students were already waiting for rides. Nothing going toward Haifa passed by. Suddenly a beautiful car appeared, going in the opposite direction. On the spur of the moment, Hannah waved

The Sea of Galilee, which Hannah visited on her day off.

it down. The driver was on his way to the village of Tiberias on the Sea of Galilee. Hannah and two of her classmates got in, and off they went—in the most luxurious car any of them had ever seen, on the most comfortable ride any of them had ever taken.

"We had barely recovered from our joy and wonder when we were already speeding towards Tiberias," Hannah wrote in an exuberant letter to her mother. "I wish a fine impressionist painter would immortalize the constantly changing vistas that emerged around each bend, each hilltop. . . . We three happy passengers constantly exchanged glances, wondering whether or not to believe our eyes as the incredible beauty of the panorama intensified. Then suddenly Nazareth appeared. Blinding-white monasteries, churches, old stone houses, Arabs, monks, nuns . . ."

The driver, an Englishman, said barely a word as the car sped along the winding roads. After a sudden turn a "wonderful blue" sprang into view: Yam Kinneret, the Sea of Galilee. "And on its shore, the town [of Tiberias], sparkling-white."

The three girls ate lunch in the park beside the lake and then set out "to see everything worth seeing." They visited the Arab quarter, where the streets were so narrow that the balconies of the houses on either side almost met overhead. They visited an Arab-Christian monastery where the garb and the faces of the inhabitants, "wreathed in white hair and long beard" were more exotic than anything Hannah had ever seen. They toured the Jewish quarter, which, though the streets were wider and the area newer, didn't differ very much from the Arab quarter. "Here, too, there is plenty of scattered orange peel decorating the streets," Hannah noted. They visited a synagogue where the benches were covered with all sorts of colored and checkered pillows, striking Hannah as truly "oriental" and almost as exotic as the monastery.

They hadn't yet begun to see everything of interest when it was time to think about returning to Nahalal. For a while, they lingered in the park, hoping to see the car that had brought them there. The English driver had said he would be going back to

Haifa late in the day and would drop them off in Nahalal en route. But neither he nor anyone else came by.

"My two classmates were beginning to get extremely worried," Hannah wrote, "but I refused to be upset." Climbing onto a mailbox, she sat in the shade and began to sing. Just then "an attractive little car" appeared, a young man at the wheel. Hannah watched her classmates wave it down—and "I then jumped from my hiding place," she wrote, "and in a moment we had installed ourselves in the three remaining seats. The poor fellow hardly knew where to put his brand new hat, which had been on the seat beside him. He hurriedly slammed the door, afraid someone else would appear."

The driver turned out to be "quite a decent chap," Hannah wrote, and the trip home to Nahalal was as pleasant as the day had been. "After the romantic beauty of the Kinneret," Hannah wrote, "the Emek stretched before us with its great fertile fields. Its beauty seems forever new, forever a thing of wonder to behold."

Two weeks later, Hannah decided to deal with "the boy question"—to bring her diary and her thoughts up to date about it. Two of the boys she had known in Hungary had written to her during the past winter. Each had asked her to marry him and each begged her to think about it before answering. "It's funny," Hannah had noted then in her diary. "They both write as if it were a very serious matter . . . [but] I didn't have to think for a moment what the answer should be . . . because they don't interest me."

Since arriving at Nahalal, several young men had befriended her. But after a short while, Hannah had broken off with each. "When I meet someone," she wrote that spring, "the thought immediately arises, perhaps this will be the real one. When I see I have been wrong I prefer breaking off completely because I can no longer go on with these little courtships. I feel that it must be a serious friendship—or let's just be forthright and say, I need a real love affair—or nothing."

Alex, a young man from Jerusalem, was very drawn to Hannah. "He proves he often thinks of me by doing delightful, thoughtful little things to please me," she wrote. "I don't know him very well yet, so don't want to pass judgment. But deep in my heart I already feel it's no. And I am sorry because I would so like it to be yes, at last."

Late spring brought a rush of wild flowers to the fields; their beauty contrasted sharply with the grim and frightening news from Europe. For the first time, Hannah wondered about the value of her work. She had come to Palestine to challenge history and to change it, but she began to feel as though she was only hiding from it. "I was sitting, studying a notebook on general agriculture," she wrote in her diary, "when suddenly I was struck by the realization of how cut off I am from the world."

It was easier for Zionists at the beginning of the movement to feel that they were doing exactly what was needed to set history right. They had believed they were creating a great and moral revolution, enabling a people who had been oppressed for centuries to resist their oppressors and take their lives into their own hands. Hannah had shared that vision, but now she began to wonder whether it was enough.

"How can I have the patience to study and prepare for an exam while the greatest war in history is raging in Europe?" she wrote. "We are witnessing . . . times which will determine the fate of man. . . . The entire world is . . . on the edge of an abyss."

In her next entry, written four days later, her turmoil was even clearer, her confusion more intense and painful. "I would like to know who and what I really am," she wrote, "but I can only ask the questions, not answer them. . . . I feel uncertain, undecided, positive and negative at one and the same time. . . . and above all, I feel so superficial that I'm ashamed to admit it even to myself."

All the voices of self-doubt descended on her at once: she questioned her judgment, the wisdom of her decision to come to

Palestine, her capacity for friendship (feeling competitive and envious of Miryam even while acknowledging how much she admired her), her feelings, her capacity for love. "My behavior toward others is so unnatural, so distant," she wrote. "I'm kind, perhaps from habit—until I'm bored with being kind. I'm capricious, fickle, supercilious; perhaps I'm rough. Is this my nature?"

Although she continued to write cheerful, reassuring letters to her mother, a sharp and growing fear for both Catherine and George began to fill Hannah's heart. "Budapest—Lyon—Nahalal," she wrote in her diary. "Between these three points my thoughts flash with lightning speed . . . I feel all the tensions of these nerve-racking days." Then the critic inside her berated her for making such a statement. "All tensions?" she continued. "I know this is a lie. I can't feel a thousandth part of what Mother must now be living through. She is suffering for our plans, dreams, which perhaps in this world holocaust will turn to ashes."

The war raged on and Hannah's fear deepened. In April 1940, the Germans unleashed their armed forces against Europe in the new and devastating style of warfare that they had already used successfully against Poland. It was called the *blitzkrieg,* the "lightning war," a sudden swift large-scale attack by Luftwaffe (air force) and Panzer (tank) divisions at once. The blitzkrieg was designed to completely overwhelm and quickly defeat an enemy, and it worked. One by one, the nations of Europe fell to the German offensive. In April, Denmark and Norway fell. In May, the Netherlands and Belgium fell and the invasion of France began. The contrast between the way the world was and the way it could be provoked a stream of unanswerable questions from Hannah.

"The sky is a brilliant blue, peace and fertility encompass the Land," she wrote on June 4, 1940. "I would like to shout into the radio, 'It isn't true! It's a lie! It's a fraud that there are a million dead and countless injured, bombings, cities destroyed! Who could have wanted this? Who can understand the historic mission of this butchery?"

Two weeks later the radio reported that the German Army

was at the gates of Paris. "Perhaps today the city will fall," Hannah wrote. "Paris and France, and the entire world. What is going to become of us?"

She longed for understanding, a perspective from which to view the war, a standpoint from which she could see when it would end, and how. "That Hitler must fall, I don't doubt," she wrote. "But how long has he been given? Fifteen years, like Napoleon? How history repeats itself. Napoleon's career, life, battles; but a twentieth-century German version turns everything into inexpressible horror."

As Hannah was writing these words, Italy entered the war as an ally of Germany—a fact "one hears a thousand times over," she recorded—bringing danger closer to Palestine than ever before. "We are preparing as much as possible," Hannah wrote. "If we are still alive 10–15 years from now, perhaps we will know why this is happening. Or perhaps it will take a hundred years before this life becomes history."

At the same time, she wrote a reassuring letter to her mother. "Everything is fine with me," Hannah began. "At the moment farm work chases away all one's dark thoughts. I'm working in the hay press, gathering the fodder, and so on. I'm brown as a berry, and the pitchfork feels as comfortable in my hand as the pen once did." She implored Catherine not to worry, and not to believe any reports she might hear about trouble in Palestine. "There is the most absolute peace here," she wrote, seemingly calm and secure. But in a diary entry written on the same day, a very different Hannah is visible: "France, George, my mother . . . ? It's difficult to say what hurts most as the days pass."

On June 21, France surrendered. Hannah could no longer write to George or receive mail from him. Although the British had finally issued his "certificate," a permit to enter Palestine, it had arrived too late. Now George could not leave France. Because Hannah had urged him to finish his schooling before coming to the Land, her critical voice chastised her unmercifully. "Oh, how awful it is to feel that I'm to blame, that I'm responsible for matters in so far as they concern George," she wrote, in great distress. "Perhaps he'll still come," she wrote hopefully, "perhaps he'll still be able to leave. I study the face of every young man, secretly hopeful."

Again and again, her thoughts turned to her mother. "I can imagine her spending sleepless nights, getting up in the morning worried, searching the newspapers, waiting for the post, locking all her worries and sadness in her heart because she is much too noble to burden others with her worries. And I, thousands of miles away, cannot sit beside her, smooth her creased brow, calm her, share the worries."

Hannah's inner turmoil did not stop, not even when she was working in the fields, not even when she was working for goals she thought were "worthy and beautiful." What right did she have to concentrate on things in the distance when there was so much suffering close at hand? Hitler's war did not yet include the Final Solution—the intention to murder all the Jews of Europe. Nevertheless its savage anti-Semitism and murderous pursuit of power made everything Hannah was doing seem trivial. How could she study and plan for the future, she asked herself, when "the entire world" was "on fire"? "The 'aye' and the 'nay' storm within me," she wrote, "the one contradicting the other."

On July 10, the German Air Force, with 2,670 front-line aircraft, attacked Great Britain in the blazing aerial assault known as the Battle of Britain. As reports of the fighting filled the airwaves, the work schedule at Nahalal came to a routine stop and the students were given a ten-day break, to do with as they pleased. Hannah and Miryam set out to travel through northern Palestine. The trip gave Hannah a chance to get some distance from the conflicts that were almost overwhelming her.

They visited Kibbutz Dan, "a little settlement, an island in the heart of a luxuriant region" where the members, mostly Transylvanian immigrants, received the girls warmly. They visited newer kibbutzim—Sasa, Dafna, Sh'ar Yashuv—which, though still primitive, had "all the requirements to develop into fertile agricultural settlements." They spent several days at Hulata, a "young collective with a charming group in a wonderful setting. . . .

An overview of the settlement at Nahalal with the fields behind it.

Excellent opportunities to swim and row. It's superfluous to add that I enjoyed myself enormously," Hannah wrote.

On their first afternoon at Kibbutz Hulata, Hannah and Miryam rowed on the Jordan River to the place where it flowed from Lake Huleh.* "The region is tropical, with papyrus reeds, water lilies, flamingoes," Hannah wrote, "and the placid green waters reflect the surrounding beauty." That evening, they went out with the kibbutz's fishing fleet. "It was a moonlit night," Hannah wrote. "The lake was absolutely calm, and the night still. We could hear only the soft and monotonous splashing of the oars. The muscular bodies of the fishermen swayed left and right in the course of their work."

During this time, Hannah felt calmer and stronger than she had in many weeks. She turned nineteen while traveling and "the entire holiday was glorious," she wrote afterward. It "strengthened my faith in the country, in myself, and in our common future. For two weeks I forgot that there is a war raging."

Kfar Gil'adi had been the girls' first stop. It was a "large,

---

*Lake Huleh no longer exists. It was drained in 1950 as part of a reclamation project that resulted in 15,000 newly fertile food-producing acres.

pleasant, orderly, well-developed" kibbutz in the northern mountains. There, in the "winds, hills, quiet," Hannah experienced again her joyous love for the Land and felt again that to be among the pioneers was to be among the blessed, those chosen by God or fate or history to do the work that would create justice on earth.

Early one morning, she set out alone to climb the hills that faced the kibbutz. "I understood why Moses received the Torah on a mountain top," she wrote later. "From there one's horizons broaden in every respect, and the order of things becomes more understandable." She exulted once again in her decision to be a pioneer and to labor for the creation of a new and just society. "In the mountains," she wrote, "one involuntarily hears the query: *'Whom shall I send?'* And the answer, *'Send me to serve the beautiful and the good!'* "

CHAPTER 6

1940-41

"How shall I grieve for them.... what can I say, and to whom?"

"ONE of my most beautiful plans," Hannah wrote in her diary in November 1940, "is to be a poultry farming instructor, to travel from one farm to another, to visit settlements, to advise and to assist, to organize, to introduce record-keeping, to develop this branch of the economy. In the evenings I would conduct brief seminars for kibbutz members, teach them the important facts of the trade. And at the same time I would get to know the people, their way of life, and would be able to travel about the country."

She chastised herself for dreaming and planning "as if there was nothing happening in the world, as if there was no war, no destruction." But that fall, the beginning of her second and final year of study at Nahalal, dream and plan she did. Another plan was to instruct children "in some sort of school," perhaps combining "agricultural work with child guidance and teaching." A third plan had to do with writing. "I want to write books, or plays, or I don't know what," she wrote in her diary. "Sometimes I think I have talent, and that it's sinful to waste or neglect it."

Working in the fields of Nahalal, Hannah contemplated the possibility of devoting her life's work to poultry farming.

No matter what specific work she did, she thought she would like to live on a kibbutz. "I'm quite sure I would fit in," she wrote, "if only the possibility of working at something that really interested me existed."

Even the chores and routine work at Nahalal were much more satisfying now than they had been the year before. She described her assignment to the bakery in August as "a joy," and in late October, in a long letter to her mother, she recounted her work with the chickens in full and loving detail. "We prepare a mixture for them all (hens, pullets and roosters) and amidst the greatest imaginable excitement I begin distributing it. I can hardly walk among the jumping white feather balls since each would like to be the first at the feeding trough. By the time I finally distribute all the feed it seems as if their necks are nailed to the troughs. They stand in double rows and won't move until every speck of food is gone. Meanwhile I fill the water dishes, gather eggs, and get extremely irritated because despite all my efforts they barely lay, since at the moment they're molting."

To her cousin Evi Sas, Hannah wrote that she had developed in the year since her arrival a "true love" for the land of Israel

Sheep grazing in a meadow of the Emek.

and had come to feel completely at home there. "I have grown to love the country, the people, the way of life, the language, and village living. I see now that even at home I was not at all a city person, lived in Budapest as if it were a village, and for that reason even here I've missed nothing of city life." Her command of Hebrew was now so good that she had begun to read Hebrew poetry. She was surprised, she wrote to Evi, that such a rich Hebrew literature existed.

Late in November 1940, the British prevented yet another refugee boat from docking in Palestine. Hoping to quiet the increasingly angry outcries of the Jewish settlers, the government claimed that there had been spies among the passengers and that they would have been a danger to Palestine's security.

"The ship sank," Hannah wrote in her diary. "Part of the passengers drowned, part were saved . . . I brood over this and ask, What is right? From a humane point of view there is no question, no doubt. One must cry out, Let them land! Haven't they . . . suffered enough? . . . But from the point of view of the country . . . really, who knows? They come from German-occupied countries. Perhaps there are elements among them likely to endanger the peace of the Land, particularly at a time when the front is drawing closer."

In discussions with other students, Hannah tried to defend the British, but she found she could not believe her own arguments. She suspected that the issue of British policy was so difficult for the Jews of Palestine to resolve because they were in a bind. Britain, "author of the White Paper," stood between them and Germany, "the representative of anti-Semitism." No matter how unfair the British were, the Jews of Palestine had to support them and accept their authority, and the British knew it. Thus they did not have to consider Jewish interests or feelings when they made their policies. They "are taking advantage of our situation," Hannah wrote. "We stand here powerless, awaiting events."

Miserable with the role the Jews of Palestine were obliged to play, Hannah tried to sort out the issues. But the restrictions of life at school left her little time to ponder important questions. She began to chafe under the rigid schedule. "They're putting out the lights," she wrote at the end of one entry. "I don't have time to explain things now. That's the way life goes on here. I don't have time to clarify these burning problems even to myself, to get any deep knowledge of the issues involved, and to reach a conclusion. I feel superficial and wanting."

In December, when another ship of refugees was turned back to sea by the British, demonstrations and protests flared throughout the Land. "The entire Jewish community unanimously demanded that they be allowed to remain in the Land," Hannah wrote. Nevertheless the ship was forced to sail away during the night. Official word was that it was heading for New Zealand. "What is there to add?" Hannah wrote. "What can we feel as human beings, as a people? And the question arises, 'How much longer?' "

Some Palestinian Jews, assessing the situation in Europe to be almost as savage and murderous as it actually was, had begun to organize rescue work as early as 1939, setting up a secret rescue center in Switzerland. When Italy entered the war, and Switzerland could no longer be used as a center of operations, a new rescue and resistance center, disguised as a business office, had been set up in Istanbul, Turkey. From there, links were created with underground and Zionist leaders in Hungary, Rumania and Bulgaria. At times the chain of communication reached into Poland itself. There was also direct contact with workers in Switzerland, who in turn had contacts in the countries of Western Europe, so that the rescue network eventually embraced the entire continent. The passionately committed people who staffed the Istanbul office infiltrated Nazi Europe as "shlichim," messengers, bringing information, money, forged identity papers, guidance and hope to individual Jews trapped there. "With infinite courage and patience they constructed the corridors through which a few might escape," wrote Marie Syrkin, who went to Palestine in 1946 to interview survivors of the Holocaust. "It was often a tedious process, always a dangerous one, and never a pretty one. Each human being wrested from the German murderers involved an enormous expenditure of money, ingenuity and daring.... Daily [the Palestinian Jews] plotted and contrived to snare the victim out of the hangman's noose.... [They] stumbled over a thousand corpses to save one living child."

The work being done from Istanbul could not, of course, be made known, not even to the Jews in Palestine. There, as the war raged on, Hannah found herself increasingly miserable and restless. Dissatisfied with everything, her work began to seem narrow and confining, her companions ordinary, her imagination dull. Even her body was something she longed to escape from. "I'd like to break out of my physical bounds," she wrote in her diary, "to fly across the fields and feel the wind in my face as I once did during a storm on my way back from the village. Running in the wind I want to cast off everyday shackles, to use words I don't use every day, to meet people I don't meet day after day."

After that entry, it was a new year—1941—before Hannah wrote in her diary again. Then it was to record that she had been ill with jaundice and was not yet completely recovered. Worse, she also had the "stabbing pains" in her heart that she had had more than a year earlier, just before leaving Hungary. Assured at that time that the cause of the pain was tension, it seemed reasonable to assume that the cause was tension now too. Still Hannah worried, as she had before, that there was something wrong with her heart. "I'm not only afraid of dying young," she wrote, "(I really do love life) but also that this may prevent me from following my chosen path and from choosing the work I like best." As before, Hannah was reluctant to consult a doctor. If the news was bad, she didn't want to hear it. "This is what is known as 'ostrich diplomacy,'" she wrote. Then as suddenly as they had begun, the stabbing pains stopped. Hannah didn't mention them again.

Meanwhile, Alex, Hannah's admirer from Jerusalem, continued to visit her at Nahalal, and to arrange excursions for himself and Hannah in the city. "There is no question at all but that he is extremely fond of me, and that he is serious about me," Hannah wrote in her diary. "But what I'm not sure about are my feelings toward him."

In February, Alex asked Hannah to marry him. "I told him that although I respect and like him, I don't feel as he does," she wrote. But she was reluctant to give the proposal a final "no," for Alex was offering her the companionship and intimacy she wanted so much and was so lonely without. He was "honest, decent and good," she noted, and she knew she could live a "pleasant simple life" with him. "The matter was left unresolved," she wrote. "He comes to see me as usual, but I asked him to wait a while before demanding a definite answer."

Hannah tried to explore her feelings for Alex in her diary. But as she pondered the future and the things she would like to do, her thoughts drifted away from him entirely. She noted that she felt "bound to some form of public service," but wondered whether a lifetime on a kibbutz would afford her the amount of personal freedom she required, the "opportunity for individual initiative and development." She thought at first that she might be able to make an important contribution in agriculture. She had, after all, already devised a number of new procedures and mechanisms for working with poultry. Then she realized that poultry farming and agriculture in general were already well-organized and that there was more need for people in government. "The general problem here is organizational," she wrote. "Political, educational, and social conditions are very disorganized, though these are exactly the areas in which our future and our fate are determined. I wonder whether I wasn't really meant to lend a helping hand in government? I've noticed at times that I have the ability to influence people, to comfort and reassure them, or to inspire them."

Suddenly, Hannah cut her diary musings short. "I started to write about Alex, and seem to have gone far afield. Perhaps therein lies the answer," she wrote. "It's difficult not to be impressed and flattered by the love of a man of character, a man you respect and esteem. But this is still not love, and thus there is really no reason to continue."

Spring came again to Palestine, Hannah's second spring in the Land. Wild flowers again covered the meadows. At night, when Hannah liked to go out walking, the stars shone brilliantly in the cloudless black sky; lights glittered warmly in the small houses that lined the lane. "Sounds of music, songs, conversation, and laughter came from all around; and far, far in the distance, I heard the barking of dogs," Hannah wrote of one April night. On that walk she felt that the houses were distant and far away, and "only the stars were near." She was filled with fear.

"Where is life leading me?" she wondered in her diary. "Will I always go on alone in the night, looking at the sparkling stars, thinking they are close? Will I be unable to hear the songs . . . the songs and the laughter around me? Will I fail to turn off the lonely road in order to enter the little houses? What must I choose? . . . When I'm among the stars I long for the small lights, and when I find my way into one of the little houses my soul yearns for the heavenly bodies."

Now, for the first time, Hannah felt that there was something unique about her restlessness, something that would not let her

Spring in the Emek.

enter the "little houses," or that would not let her stay. She could not identify the source of her restlessness, or its meaning. She only knew that she felt pulled, possibly even chosen, to follow a solitary path. "Sometimes I feel I am an emissary who has been entrusted with a mission," she wrote. "What this mission is—is not clear to me. . . . I feel I have a duty toward others, as if I were obligated to them. At times this appears to be all sheer nonsense, and I wonder why all this individual effort . . . and why particularly me?"

As Hannah pondered and searched for a course of action, the blitzkrieg in Europe continued. Before April was over, Yugoslavia had fallen to the Germans and the German Army had begun its advance through Greece. There was fighting now in Libya, and no one could say how long it would be before that country too fell to the Germans. The front was closer to the Land than it had ever been, and Palestine, Hannah wrote, "is deadlocked in weakness, misunderstanding and lack of purpose." Everyone in

Palestine was discussing politics, but, Hannah noted, "no one dares to ask: What will happen if the Germans come here?" The words might seem meaningless on paper, Hannah noted, "but if we close our eyes and listen only to our hearts, we hear the pounding of fear."

Would the Jewish homeland survive? "It's dreadful to contemplate the possibility of its end at close hand," Hannah wrote. "And though everyone wants to be hopeful, to reassure himself, deep within is submerged the thought that perhaps . . ." She did not finish the sentence.

Again Hannah complained of the lack of unity among the settlers, the lack of organization, the absence of a leader who could pull everyone together and help them face the enemy. "There is no one to say, 'Enough!' No one to whom they will listen. I feel a deep sense of responsibility," she wrote. "Perhaps I ought to say the word!"

Although Hannah realized this thought was farfetched, she couldn't dismiss it easily. She saw the overwhelming need that existed, and she felt a corresponding need in herself to be of use. Her feelings traveled back and forth between what she felt she could really do, and what needed to be done. "Even if I had the courage to rise up and speak," she wrote, "they wouldn't listen to me. Who and what am I to assume such a task? I can't do this, of course. But to do nothing, merely to look on from afar—that I can't do either." The dangers her people faced from the "butchers of Europe" demanded action. But what action could she take? "As if in a nightmare," Hannah wrote, "I would like to scream, but no voice comes from my throat; I'd like to run, but my legs lack the strength. I can't come to terms with the thought that everything must be lost, destroyed, without us having the slightest say or influence on the course of things. I want to believe that the catastrophe won't come to pass," she concluded. "But if it does, I hope we'll face it with honor. And if we can't hold out, that we will fall honorably."

Hannah wondered what would make a death honorable. A

death chosen in order to consecrate God's name? Could one even consecrate God's name in a way that was divorced from life itself? Was there anything more holy than life? She ended her musing without coming to any conclusion. "It's three o'clock," she wrote. "I must go to work."

About this time, Hannah wrote another poem. It is called simply "To Die."

> To die . . . so young to die . . . no, no, not I.
> I love the warm sunny skies,
> Light, songs, shining eyes.
> I want no war, no battle cry—
> No, no . . . Not I.
>
> But if it must be that I live today
> With blood and death on every hand,
> Praised be He for the grace, I'll say
> To live, if I should die this day . . .
> Upon your soil, my home, my land.

Hannah noted the tentativeness that had crept into people's conversations. They made plans, discussed what they were going to do, and then added, "If, meanwhile . . ." Although the sentence was never finished, everyone knew that the reference was to a German invasion, and the possibility of their own imminent death. "I feel I still have a lot to do in this life, and that I cannot die before doing it all," she wrote. "Our entire young country, filled with love and the will to live, feels this way."

By the middle of June 1941, Greece had fallen to the Germans. The island of Crete had fallen too, and there was large-scale fighting going on in nearby Egypt and Syria. The cities of Haifa and Tel Aviv were both being bombed. In Nahalal, people could hear the bombs exploding in Haifa and the firing of the gunners on the ground. "It looks now as if the war is starting here," Hannah wrote in her diary.

—79—

Now, in a poem she entitled "For the Brothers," Hannah acknowledged that others might have to finish the work she and the people with her had started. In somber words, she implored them to continue.

> Should we break,
> Then take the burden
> Heavy and great
> Upon you.
>
> Build upon sand
> Under the blue
> Sky . . . everything
> Anew.
>
> And know, costly
> The road to the just
> And the true.

On June 22, 1941, Germany invaded Russia. There, according to the radio reports Hannah heard, the "fiercest battles since the beginning of the war" were being waged. Tension in Palestine mounted. "Everyone knows the results of this struggle will be decisive to the future of the world," Hannah wrote.

In July, a group of refugees from Poland managed to make their way to Palestine, bearing stories of Jews in their native land being forced from their homes and expelled from their villages; of Jews—even children and babies—being rounded up and shot en masse; of cities where Jews were being herded into small sections, denied medical treatment, denied food, prevented from leaving or even communicating with the outside world; of camps in the countryside where thousands were imprisoned and unknown numbers were dying from starvation and disease. Unknown, even to them, was the fact that in the middle of July, the construction of death camps at secluded sites in Poland had begun.

In early July, Hannah received a frantic telegram from Catherine, who had heard about the bombings of Palestine and was desperate at the thought that Hannah might be in danger. The telegram filled Hannah with anguish. "It's awful to think that while I'm living a normal, comfortable, peaceful life, Mother is worried sick," she wrote in her diary, "envisioning me in all sorts of frightful situations, allowing herself no peace." Even worse, she felt it wasn't fair for her to be safe while others were in danger. "I'm conscience-stricken that I have it so good and easy here while others are suffering," she wrote, "and feel I ought to do something—something exerting, demanding—to justify my existence."

Toward the end of August, the students at Nahalal were given time to tour the countryside and visit the kibbutzim and villages in which they might like to live. Their course of study was drawing to a close and they would be leaving Nahalal in September. Hannah visited several settlements, and spent a week in Jerusalem where the Hebrew University offered a week-long seminar on poultry ailments. But she returned to Nahalal still undecided about where she would go or what she would do when she graduated. "Everyone asks me what my plans are, and they're amazed I haven't made a decision yet," she wrote. She wasn't worried, however. "I'll find the right answer when the time comes."

On September 1, 1941, at the graduation ceremony, Hannah presented the farewell speech in the name of her class at Nahalal. "Our road was not an easy one," she said. "It was filled with obstacles, contradictions, misunderstandings. There were also differences of opinion. And we still don't know . . . how well we'll stand the rigors of a life of work, a life which will demand our best possible efforts, and all the knowledge and preparation we acquired here. If we can fulfill all the demands the working settlement will impose upon us we'll prove to the school and to ourselves that we really benefitted from our two years here. One thing we know already: we're going out to do peaceful battle, to work. And we're armed with a valuable weapon: a knowledge of agriculture."

She thanked Hanna Meisel, the director of the school, as well as the teachers, counselors, "and the entire region for unconsciously teaching us by the example of their daily lives and the Hebrew atmosphere they provided." Finally, she thanked the parents of the students for "willingly, unselfishly" letting their daughters go, "so we could stand up in life with heads held high. Words alone cannot thank them," she said. "If our work and our lives prove a blessing to our surroundings, and satisfying to ourselves—that will be our thanks."

With graduation behind her, Hannah set out to hitchhike through the north of Palestine, staying at one kibbutz, then another, watching, trying to find the right place for her. At the end of September, on the eve of Rosh Hashanah, Hannah was at a kibbutz called Ness Tziyona. Alone with her thoughts as night fell, she acknowledged her loneliness and her confusion. Two years had passed since she had last seen her mother. If she could talk to her now, what would she say? "I would tell her how I felt yesterday," Hannah wrote in her diary. "I was so desperately depressed that I cried. I felt I was faced with two possibilities: to seek personal happiness and shut my eyes to all the problems in the world or else to invest my efforts in the difficult and devastating war for the things I deem good and proper."

For the people who were suffering at that very moment, Hannah could not find words or consolation. What could she do, what did she have to offer? "How shall I grieve for them on the Eve of Rosh Hashanah?" she wrote. "About the suffering, the pain; the injustice . . . what can I say, and to whom?"

She did not have a clear or consistent belief in the personal God of traditional religion. "For me He is more a symbol and expression of the moral forces in which I believe," she wrote. Nevertheless, on this Rosh Hashanah she beseeched God as fervently as the most devout believer. "If You've kindled a fire in my heart," she wrote, "allow me to burn that which should be burned in my house—the House of Israel. . . . give me, as well, the strength to scourge, to caress, to uplift. And grant that these words be not empty phrases, but a credo for my life. Toward what am I aiming? Toward all that which is best in the world, and of which there is a spark within me."

CHAPTER 7

1941-43

"We awaited you two thousand years"

IN December 1941, the month the United States entered the war, Hannah found the kibbutz she wished to join. It did not have a permanent home yet, but it did have a site picked out on the coast of the Mediterranean Sea, halfway between Tel Aviv and Haifa, near the ruins of the ancient city of Caesarea. Built by the Roman King Herod in 22 B.C.E., Caesarea had been splendid—with a limestone sea wall 200 feet wide, colossal statues lining the harbor, a temple of exceptional size and beauty, a vast drainage system operated by tidal power, a theater, an amphitheater and a hippodrome that could seat 20,000 people. Rivaling even Jerusalem in its day, Caesarea had been a magnificent outpost of the Roman Empire in the land of the Jews. When Hannah saw the site, she thought it was magical, "enchanting." She felt that something "great" was going to begin there.

The doubts and reservations that had kept her traveling from one kibbutz to another throughout the fall, unable to make a commitment, were not entirely gone. "I'm still intrigued by that unconscious, hesitant voice that says, 'Perhaps you shouldn't,' "

The ruins at Caesarea near the site of Sdot-Yam.
Hannah thought the spot "enchanting."

she wrote after arriving at Kibbutz Sdot-Yam—the Fields of the Sea—and asking to be accepted as a candidate for membership. Sometimes she felt as though there was a "fire within" her. And a voice inside her cautioned her against "wasting" her abilities—tying herself to a situation that would not be demanding enough, or not demanding in the right way. The newness of Kibbutz Sdot-Yam appealed to Hannah very much. She would have a chance to help create it from the ground up. In addition, most of the members were Sabras, born in the Land, as different from Hannah as they could be. These were people from whom she felt she could learn a lot. In the end, however, it was the site itself that convinced her. She wrote this poem after her first visit there.

Hush, cease all sound.
Across the sea is the sand,
The shore known and near,
The shore, golden, dear,
Home, the Homeland.

With step twisting and light
Among strangers we move,
Word and song hushed
Toward the future-past
Caesarea . . .

But reaching the city of ruins
Soft a few words we intone.
We return. We are here.
Soft answers the silence of stone,
We awaited you two thousand years.

A handful of kibbutz members were already living at the selected site, preparing it for the arrival of the others. But the majority—almost eighty in all—were living in temporary quarters farther up the coast on the outskirts of Haifa. Some of them were housed in wooden huts, most in tents. Hannah arrived in mid-winter, and conditions at the settlement were as harsh as any she had ever experienced.

"I'll try to write a bit, though my hands are nearly frozen," she wrote in her diary on January 2, 1942, a little more than a week after her arrival. "Outside—a fearful storm. Five tents were blown down during the night. Ours didn't collapse, but the wind is howling around it on all sides, sand has covered everything, and my bed is rocking ceaselessly with a monotonous beat."

She did not continue that entry, but later in the day, began another. "I've wrapped one rag on top of another around myself and am now in one of the rooms, since it's impossible to remain in the tent. I want to write about the past year. Without noticing, we stepped into 1942." For the rest of the entry, though, she only recorded her sinking spirits. "It is a gray, rainy day that depresses one's very soul," she wrote, "and though the rain doesn't penetrate the room, it robs me of the incentive to do anything. . . . It's hard to imagine that spring and sunshine will come again."

The community at Haifa was not self-supporting, and to earn money, some of the members worked on the docks, and some hired themselves out as household laborers. Hannah worked as a laundress. "It's difficult for me to write," she wrote at the end of one day's work. "My hands are nearly frozen after a day of washing." She felt peculiar to be serving in a private home, "and as a laundress at that—the meanest of all forms of housework." But she also felt proud. She hadn't been driven to this work by necessity—she had chosen it freely for idealistic reasons. And though nothing in her life had prepared her for it, she was doing it, and doing it well. "I was in a wonderful mood all the way home, singing and laughing," she wrote after a day spent working as a laundress off the kibbutz. "There was a feeling of enormous satisfaction in knowing that if I must I can do even that."

Hannah had chosen Sdot-Yam in part because the members were not like her. However, this seemed less and less to be a plus as the weeks went by, for Hannah found herself feeling more and more shut out and lonely. A visit from Miryam not long after Hannah's arrival at Sdot-Yam highlighted this sense of isolation. "She's the only person in the Land with whom I can discuss everything that concerns me," Hannah wrote, "and who understands. Sometimes I look about me and realize how very much alone I am among my colleagues and acquaintances."

Early in February, Hannah visited the Sdot-Yam site at Caesarea for the second time. She strolled among the ancient ruins and walked through the fields—or what would one day be the fields of the kibbutz. She was more enchanted with the setting than ever, with "the infinite horizon, the sea . . . As one sits by the sea one thinks of the world's past," she wrote, "and contemplates its future; one's scope broadens, one's determination to achieve something great and beautiful strengthens."

Nevertheless, life at the Haifa settlement did not become any easier. Soon added to Hannah's feeling of distance between herself and the other members was the impression that they actively disliked her. "I spoke up at several meetings and discussions," Hannah wrote soon after her return from Caesarea. "Now I'm very sorry. I'm sure most of the members see this as a desire to be conspicuous, which won't make my acceptance by the group any easier. It's always more difficult to mend fences than to break them."

It isn't possible to know whether or not Hannah's perceptions were correct. Certainly, her background was very different from that of the other members of the kibbutz. She had been raised in a well-to-do, sophisticated family in a cosmopolitan capital of Europe. By contrast, the others were the rugged children of pioneers and farmers. Perhaps they *did* think badly of her. Perhaps they felt ill at ease. Hannah, in any case, believed they disliked her. In general, she thought that other people's "estimations" of her "character" usually passed through three stages. "The first impression is very good, but entirely wrong," she wrote. "In this one I include all superficial acquaintanceships and unwanted visitors. In the second phase, the impression takes a turn for the worse; and in the third phase, they get to know me as I really am. But not many get that far."

In all the Land, Hannah thought, only Miryam had reached that third stage. The members of Sdot-Yam, Hannah was certain, were in the second phase. It's difficult to believe that this assessment was correct, but she was convinced that it was. "It's hard to explain the basis for my feelings," she wrote, "but I sense a coldness, and a lack of trust. . . . either they think I'm very naïve or take me for a chatterbox who arrogantly talks big about things she can never realize. They think my initial enthusiasm and activity will wane as I encounter reality. Naturally, no one has said any of this to me, but I'm sensitive enough to feel it." She ended this entry by noting that on that February day, she had washed 150 pairs of socks. "I thought I'd go mad."

That January in Poland, where three and a half million Jews

were living at the time of the German invasion, the first of Hitler's death camps was opened. Designed to kill and burn the bodies of hundreds of people at a time, several times a day, day after day, for an indefinite, extended period, the camp was opened at a place called Chelmno in western Poland. At the same time, far to the north, in the once lovely city of Vilna, the "Jerusalem of Lithuania," the first resistance organization of the war was formed. It was called the United Partisans Organization, and it was led by a twenty-two-year-old poet named Abba Kovner.

Members of the United Partisans Organization pose for a photograph.
Abba Kovner, the founder, is the young man in the center.

It was in Poland, where Jews had lived for over 700 years, that Hitler had decided to concentrate all the Jews of Europe. The decision to murder them all may not have been made in 1939, when Poland was invaded. Most historians believe that decision was made sometime in 1940 or 1941. Until then, Hitler may not have had a plan for the Jews beyond isolating them, gathering them in one area so that the rest of Europe would be *Judenrein* —"clean of Jews." But his government's intention to murder as many Jews as possible was clear from the beginning of the invasion.

"We Germans face a two-fold fight today," stated an indoctrination booklet published early in 1939 for use by the German Army. "With regard to the non-Jewish people we want only to conduct a chivalrous argument with them. But we fight world Jewry as one has to fight a poisonous parasite; we encounter in him not only the enemy of our people but a plague of all peoples. The fight against Jewry is a moral fight for the purity and health of God-created humanity and for a more just order in the world."

Massacres of Jews had been carried out in 1939 by the Einsatzgruppen, the "Special Duty Forces" that followed the German Army into Poland. A paramilitary police force, the Einsatzgruppen's special task was said to be "security." In practice, their job was to kill all civilians who were perceived to be a danger to Germany. They killed non-Jewish Poles by the thousands. But their special targets were Jews. They shot Jewish people at random in the streets and in their homes. They ordered Jews to gather in the marketplace and then fired into the crowd. Jews were beaten to the ground and set on fire. They were hung from trees and boiling water was poured over them. In one town, the rabbi was decapitated and his head displayed in the window of a shop for days. The atrocities committed against Jews shocked even some German generals.

Poland had been overrun by the German Army in less than a month. By October 1939, the government and all governmental functions were under the control of the Nazis. All surviving Jews were expelled from their homes and villages and forced to make their way to the cities in central Poland, an area the Germans called the General Government. There they were crowded into *ghettoes:* small, usually rundown sections that were walled off and guarded by soldiers. Because of a pact between Germany and the Soviet Union, eastern Poland was ruled by Russia until June 1941, when Germany broke the pact and invaded Russia and Russian-occupied Poland. Then the Jews of eastern Poland too

*German soldiers occupy
a Polish village
during the Blitzkrieg,
1939.*

*Polish Jewish children during a Nazi action. Their parents may have been taken
away and the children left to fend for themselves.*

Polish Jews forced to flee their homes by the Nazis.

were brutalized and murdered, the survivors removed to ghettoes.

It was the German government's official policy to allow as many Jews as possible to die of starvation in the ghettoes. The name for this policy was *Hungertod:* literally, death by hunger. Food rations were deliberately inadequate, and the smuggling of edibles became a heroic, lifesaving activity. But in spite of it, people died by the hundreds and thousands of starvation. Those whom hunger did not kill, it debilitated. Epidemic and crowd diseases raged, brought on by the weakness and frailty of the half-starved people and the filthy conditions in which they were forced to live. One-fifth of the Jews of Poland, 700,000 people, died of starvation and disease in the ghettoes. An anonymous ghetto poem recorded this misery.

> When we had nothing to eat
> They gave us a turnip, they gave us a beet.
> Here, have some grub, have some fleas.
> Have some typhus. Die of disease.

By December 1941, only 12,000 of the original 60,000 Jews of the Vilna ghetto remained alive; 18,000 had died of starvation or disease; 30,000 had been killed outright by the Gestapo, the secret state police force of Nazi Germany, whose members were encouraged to be brutal and sadistic—so much so that they frequently fought even with one another. Members of the Gestapo had full police powers to seize, arrest and execute, but their job had nothing to do with maintaining order or preventing crime. The Gestapo was a terror squad. Its job was to create fear in civilian populations and to eliminate—by killing them—everyone who opposed or questioned Hitler's regime. In the Vilna ghetto, members of the Gestapo rounded up groups of Jews almost daily, announcing that they were to be resettled elsewhere. The people, young and old, alone and in families, were loaded onto trucks and driven out of the ghetto. Perhaps they hoped conditions would be better where they were going. Twenty miles outside of Vilna, in a wooded area called Ponary, they were killed.

On the last day of December, one of the people taken to Ponary was a schoolteacher named Tema Katz who, shot and left for dead, had climbed out of the burial pit and made her way back to the ghetto and to the quarters of Abba Kovner. A meeting was called for January 1 at which Tema told the truth about Ponary. Afterward, Kovner issued a call for self-defense:

"Jewish youth," Kovner said, "do not believe those who are trying to deceive you. Those who are taken out of the gates of the ghetto will never return. All the Gestapo's roads lead to Ponary, and Ponary means death.

"Comrades! Let us defend ourselves! Even if we are deprived of the possibility of an armed defense in this unequal contest of strength, we nevertheless can still defend ourselves!

"Convey your hatred of the foe in every place and at every moment!

"Better to fall in the fight for human dignity than to live at the mercy of the murderer!"

The young women and men at the meeting that night became

the core of the United Partisans Organization. They faced a murderous, well-armed, well-fed army. And they faced a heart-wrenching choice: should they try to escape from the ghetto, make their way to the forests, and fight the Germans from there, or should they remain in the ghetto and help the people who could not escape prepare for the day the Germans would come to get them? Most of the young fighters in Vilna, like the fighters in the other ghettoes of Eastern Europe, chose to remain in the ghetto and prepare for its defense, though they knew such a defense was not practical: in a fight against the German army they would not win. They fought, therefore, not for life but for honor and for vengeance. "We are going on the road to death, remember that," said Aaron Liebeskind, a member of the underground in the Polish city of Krakow. "Whoever desires still to live should not search for life here among us. We are at the end." "We'll kill our slaughterers, they will have to fall together with us," wrote an underground fighter in the Polish city of Bialystok. In a letter to friends in Palestine that never reached them, for it could not be mailed, she exhorted them to continue the fight. "We call you to vengeance, revenge without remorse or mercy . . . Vengeance! This is our challenge to you, who have not suffered in Hitler's hell."

That spring in Palestine, a call went out urging young settlers to join the Palmach, the Jewish commando unit created in 1941 to defend the Land. The Palmach was the striking unit of the Haganah, the Jewish self-defense force created in the 1920s when the settlers realized they could not rely on the British to protect them. When the British outlawed the Haganah in the 1930s and forbade it to purchase weapons of any kind, the organization went underground. As the war came closer to the Middle East, however, the British unofficially solicited and received help from the Haganah time and time again. Senior Haganah officers advised the British, scouted and prepared lists of bridges and roads in Lebanon, Syria, Turkey and Iran that could be sabotaged in case of a German invasion. In the early spring of 1941, when German tank divisions were dispatched to the Middle East, and the Nazis

Young members of the Haganah arrested by British soldiers.

began to infiltrate Syria, the Haganah, with the silent permission of the British, created the Palmach. This unit also met British requests for scouts, guides and saboteurs. In June 1941, during the Allied invasion of Syria, members of the Palmach guided Allied soldiers, ambushed enemy patrols, sabotaged roads. In the spring of 1942, as the hard-driving German Afrika Korps was pressing toward Cairo and the Suez Canal, the British began to fortify northern Palestine and to actively increase the fighting power of the Jewish soldiers. Additional weapons were obtained for the Palmach, and the drive to recruit new members was intensified.*

"Many girls can't join the army," Hannah wrote in her diary. "Those who can, who have no family ties, ought to join." At a general kibbutz meeting, she proposed herself as a candidate for recruitment. The members agreed to recommend her, and Hannah was very pleased at the "decent behavior of the settlement" toward her. For the first time, she felt the members trusted her.

---

*Once the Germans were hurled back at El Alamein, and the danger to Palestine ebbed, the British confiscated the weapons. Palmach units thereupon broke into the British arsenal and "confiscated" them back.

Later that spring, the first official descriptions of the Einsatzgruppen's actions in Poland reached the West. A Jewish group in Warsaw had managed to get word through the lines to the Polish government-in-exile in London, which released the shocking descriptions. People found the reports of atrocities and mass murders "difficult to believe," though at that very moment in Russia, the Einsatzgruppen were still performing their "special tasks." One of the stories that eventually reached the West told what the Einsatzgruppen did in August 1942 in the town of Zagrodski. All the Jews, about 500 families, had been ordered to the village square for a roll call. Then trucks arrived. Armed soldiers commanded everyone to climb aboard. Those who could not fit on the trucks were ordered to run behind. Those who fell or stumbled along the way were shot. With her daughter in her arms, Rivka Yosselescka was one of the people who had to run. Here is part of the story she told later.

"When I came to the place where the trucks had brought the others, they were lined up and naked," Rivka said. "Some of the young people tried to run, but they were caught immediately and they were shot right there. . . . I felt [the SS man] try to take my child from my arms. The child cried out and was shot immediately. . . . Then he aimed at me and fired. I fell to the ground into the pit amongst the bodies. I felt a sort of heaviness and I thought I was dead, that this was the feeling which comes after death. Then I felt that I was choking; people were falling over me. . . . and then I felt that I was climbing. . . . I came out on top of the grave, and when I did, I did not know the place, so many bodies were lying all over, dead people; I wanted to see the end of this stretch of dead bodies but I could not. . . ."

The Germans were gone by then and Rivka searched among the bodies for her daughter. Then as she watched from the edge of the forest, the Germans returned and filled the pit with earth. When they left, she made her way back to the grave. "I was praying for death to come," she recalled. "I was praying for the grave to be opened and to swallow me alive. Blood was spurting from the grave in many places, like a well of water, and whenever I pass a spring now, I remember the blood which spurted from the ground, from that grave. I was digging with my fingernails, trying to join the dead in that grave, but the grave would not open. I did not have enough strength. I cried out to my mother, to my father, 'Why did they not kill me too? What was my sin?'

"And I remained there, stretched out on the grave, three days and three nights."

Later that same month, 2,000 miles from Zagrodski, Hannah heard on the radio that the Germans were approaching the city of Alexandria, Egypt. She waited anxiously for word from the Palmach. Meanwhile, she received a short note from her mother in which Catherine assured her that she was well, "only," she added, "my hair has turned a bit gray." "I've never longed for her the way I long for her now," Hannah wrote in her diary. "I'm so overwhelmed with this need for her at times, and with the constant fear that I'll never see her again. I wonder, can I bear it?"

Rosh Hashanah, September 1942, came and went. Hannah made no note of it. During this time, she was accepted as a full member of Kibbutz Sdot-Yam. Immediately, she asked to be transferred from the Haifa settlement to the working crew in Caesarea. Her transfer was approved. "I know the difficulties in advance," she wrote, "a small group, completely unsuitable. But I may find my place among them."

She did not. Lonely and dispirited, she walked for hours along the beaches of the settlement, pondering, wishing, trying to salvage what she could of her faith in herself, in the Land, in the future. A short, simple poem, "Walk to Caesarea," was written about this time.

> God—may there be no end
> to sea, to sand,
> water's splash,
> lightning's flash
> the prayer of man

Her diary entries now were sporadic; those few she made were glum and sadly out of focus. "The long pauses," she noted, "are indicative of my situation. Sometimes there's no ink in my pen; sometimes I don't have a light; sometimes it's noisy . . . and sometimes I have no reason to write. Sometimes I don't have time to write, and sometimes I don't feel like writing. Not because nothing happens . . . But I've simply been apathetic to everything that's been going on." In her poem "A Glance," Hannah sounded a note almost of defeat.

> How far, far have the people lagged,
> Infinitely far have the seas receded.
> How distant now the gay and dancing times,
> How languid the once proud songs and rhymes,
> How distant . . . How languid . . .

At Caesarea, there was no one to whom she felt close or to whom she felt she could turn. "I live in a world of my own making, without any contact with the outside world," she wrote. "I live here like a drop of oil on water, sometimes afloat, sometimes submerged, but always remaining apart, never mixing with another drop."

She longed for her family. "I can think of nothing now but my mother and brother," she wrote in early January 1943. "I am sometimes overwhelmed by dreadful fears. Will we ever meet again?"

Painfully lonely, she grew short-tempered; there was a harsh edge to her impatience that had not been there before. Asked to serve as storekeeper for the little settlement, for example, she complained angrily. "It's a pity to waste more years of energy and strength on something I so dislike doing, and which will hinder my development in other directions," she wrote. She was ashamed of herself for complaining, but couldn't "rid" herself of "the belief that precious years are being wasted."

She reserved most of her anger, however, for herself. Diary entries reveal her losing patience even with her own unhappiness, losing sympathy for her own feelings of isolation. "I hear singing from the dining hall," she wrote at the Haifa settlement, to which she had returned for a visit when the winter was almost over. "A party . . . I have no desire to join them. I've nothing to do there. I don't know what to do when I'm with people." Then she admonished herself. "Nonsense!" she wrote. "The same gripe again. I don't know what's wrong with me. Loneliness is difficult, but so is contact with people." Her list of complaints included many things, but her impatience with herself was chief among them. "I don't like my work, and I'm annoyed that it takes up all my time. It's not worth writing about. If I could only organize my thoughts. But I've stopped thinking."

As December turned to January, Hannah had been in agony —afraid of what might lie in store for Palestine, heartsick for her mother and brother in Europe. In spite of her best intentions, it seemed, she had failed to do what was needed. And now, like the young resistance fighters of Europe, she was faced with impossible choices. Should she stay in Palestine, in the Land she had come to love, the only place on earth that promised a just future for her people? What about the ones who could not come, the ones who were trapped in Europe and might be doomed to die there? What about her mother? How could Hannah not be among them at this time? If they could not escape, how could she not go to them and try to help?

On the eighth day of January 1943, Hannah's confusion suddenly ended. After a "shattering" week, she suddenly knew exactly what she must do: return to Hungary. She must help the people who were trapped there to escape. She must find her mother and bring her to Palestine. Although "I'm quite aware how absurd the idea is," she wrote, "it still seems both feasible and necessary to me, so I'll get to work on it and carry it through."

"We awaited you two thousand years," the sun-drenched stones of Caesarea had seemed to say to her. But Hannah could not stay.

Caesarea.

CHAPTER 8

1943-44

"I see everything that has happened to me so far as preparation and training for the mission ahead"

ALMOST a month and a half after Hannah's decision to return to Hungary, a young Palmach man named Yonah Rosen visited the settlement at Caesarea. Hannah had met him two years earlier when she was making the rounds of kibbutzim and had stopped briefly at his kibbutz, Ma'agan, on the Sea of Galilee. Most of the members there, like Rosen himself, were Hungarian. That was one of the reasons Hannah had chosen not to stay. But now, in February of 1943, she felt drawn to him, as to close kin. He too had left his family in Hungary when he came to Palestine. And he too was tormented by fears for them. Now he told Hannah that at Palmach Headquarters, which were being set up at his kibbutz, a rescue mission to Europe was being discussed. The idea was to drop parachutists behind the lines into the German-occupied countries. They would have to be natives of the countries to which they were sent so they could mix easily with the people and not arouse suspicion. Their job would be to help organize resistance to the Germans and to lead out the Jews who were trapped there. Rosen had already asked to be on the

Hungarian mission. Hannah told him that was exactly what she wanted to do.

"I was truly astounded," Hannah wrote in her diary. "The *identical* idea! My answer, of course, was that I'm absolutely ready."

Rosen explained that the mission was not yet a sure thing. Haganah leaders had been trying for years to persuade the British to help organize a rescue mission to Eastern Europe. The British had never been interested. They didn't think such a mission would help the general war effort—"just the Jews." But toward the end of January 1943, the Allied Air Command had sent bombers to destroy the Ploesti oil refineries of Rumania. Hundreds of Allied airmen—many more than had been anticipated —had been shot down and captured, making it clear that the Allies needed more and better information about German defenses in the area. Suddenly the idea of a parachute mission began to make sense to the British. Many Palestinian Jews were from the Balkan countries, including Rumania. They knew the languages of the area, the people and the terrain. They would be able to act as spies, gather information, contact underground groups and set up escape routes for the captured airmen. If they would do this first, and then go about the work of helping the Jews, the British said they would be willing to train them and supply the weapons, parachutes and airplanes. There was much resentment among Haganah leaders about the order of priorities, and much suspicion among the British about the reliability of the Jews. But it seemed as though an agreement might soon be reached. Yonah promised to let Hannah know how things developed. He thought she was "admirably suited" for the mission.

"I see the hand of destiny in this," Hannah wrote in her diary, "just as I did at the time of my Aliyah. I wasn't master of my fate then either. I was enthralled by one idea, and it gave me no rest. I knew I would emigrate, despite the many obstacles in my path. Now I again sense the excitement of something important and vital ahead, and the feeling of inevitability connected with a decisive and urgent step." She didn't know whether or not the people in charge would accept her. "But I think I have the capabilities necessary for just this assignment," she wrote, "and I'll fight for it with all my might."

Now her old enthusiasm returned. "I can't sleep at night," she wrote a few days after Yonah Rosen's visit, "because of the scenes I envisage: how I'll conduct myself in this or that situation . . . how I'll notify Mother of my arrival . . . how I'll organize the Jewish Youth."

Two months later, on the first night of Passover, the holiday that marks the ancient exodus of the Jews from slavery in Egypt, an all-night vigil was set up among the Jews in the ghetto in Warsaw, Poland. They had been informed through contacts in the underground that the Germans were going to attack the ghetto at dawn. Sandbags and pillows were placed on window-sills. Doorways and entranceways to houses were barricaded with furniture. Weapons were distributed; fighting units took up positions. Food was distributed, and poison.

At two A.M. the Polish police, German police, Lithuanian and Ukrainian SS Auxiliary forces threw a ring around the ghetto. Every twenty-five feet there was a guard with a heavy machine gun. At three A.M. Gestapo Chief Brandt drove through the ghetto in his black limousine. Everything was in order.

At dawn, the Germans attacked. They had chosen this day, April 19, to destroy the ghetto as a birthday present for Hitler, who would be fifty-four the next day. The Germans knew there was an underground in the ghetto, that it was armed, and that it would offer resistance. So they had prepared 2,009 armed SS soldiers; three detachments of the Wehrmacht, including artillery, tanks, flamethrowers, armored cars and mine-sappers; 234 soldiers and officers of the German police; 360 soldiers and officers of the Polish police; 35 members of the Security Police; 337 Ukrainian and Lithuanian Nazis, including enlisted men and officers.

The German attack was stopped immediately when members of the Jewish Fighting Organization, numbering about 600, met it with grenades and bottled explosives—"Molotov cocktails."

The JFO had been formed the previous summer, when it was learned that the Germans intended to evacuate the ghetto completely and send all the people to their deaths in a nearby camp called Treblinka. Three hundred thousand people had been taken from the ghetto by then, believing, as the Germans told them, that they were going to be "resettled in work camps in the east." The truth had been discovered when a young Jew, who was blond and fair and could pass easily for a Gentile, secretly followed the route taken by ghetto trains and discovered a special spur off the main track. The spur led to Treblinka. He did not enter the camp, but learned from a contact in the village that the Jews who were brought there were killed immediately. His report was published in an underground newspaper and a month later confirmed by the report of a man who had escaped from Treblinka itself. His job there had been to help dispose of the corpses, and he described the grisly death camp in detail.

The Polish underground press distributed 2,000 copies of these reports and sent a microfilm of it to the Polish government-in-exile in London and to the United States. In the ghetto itself,

Nazis round up people in the Warsaw ghetto. They told them they were to be resettled. In fact, they were taken to Treblinka death camp.

fighting units were formed and a desperate search for weapons began. The JFO also plastered the walls of the ghetto with signs telling the truth about Treblinka and urging the people not to go when they were called for "resettlement." Jews began to go into hiding. They rioted when they were rounded up. They were massacred in the streets. People were dragged from their homes, beaten to the ground and hurled onto the trains. Throughout the ghetto, scattered acts of sabotage were carried out. Factories were set on fire, warehouse windows smashed, soldiers ambushed. In December 1942, a JFO group overcame the guards at a ghetto prison and freed 100 Jews. In January, four days of fighting raged between Jews and Germans in an action that electrified the ghetto. Twenty Germans were killed in what was an enormous victory for the poorly equipped, half-starved Jewish fighters. Their entire arsenal at this time consisted of 143 revolvers, one machine pistol, and seven rounds of ammunition. In February, another armed clash took place. Then the German High Command ordered the Warsaw ghetto destroyed.

On the morning of April 19, 1943, when the first Germans

Family killed by Nazis in the rubble of the Warsaw ghetto.
They may have resisted a roundup.

to enter the ghetto were met with explosives, they panicked and fled, leaving their dead and wounded behind. They returned shortly with reinforcements, but were quickly turned away a second time. The first battle of what would become known as the Warsaw Ghetto Uprising had begun at six A.M. It was over two hours later. Victory went to the Jews.

The second battle began at noon. This time the Germans entered the ghetto like snipers. Hugging the buildings as they moved and protecting themselves with a barrage of artillery fire, they rendered the Jews' grenades and Molotov cocktails almost useless. Unable to maintain their positions, the Jews maneuvered over the rooftops, throwing grenades as they ran. Then General Jurgen von Stroop, commanding the German forces, called in airplanes, forcing the Jews to leave the rooftops. Before retreating, they set fire to a large German warehouse. In retaliation, the Germans bombarded and set fire to the ghetto hospital, threw the sick into the flames and killed newborn infants with their bare hands.

On April 20, Hitler's birthday, the Germans demanded that the resistance fighters lay down their weapons and surrender—otherwise the ghetto would be razed. The demand was refused. Outside the ghetto, the Polish People's Guard, a tiny band of underground resistance fighters, tried to help. They attacked one of the German artillery emplacements that was bombarding Jewish positions near the ghetto wall. The four soldiers who made up the artillery crew were all killed and the guns silenced. With its small membership and limited supply of weapons, this action was all the People's Guard could undertake. The Armia Krajowa, the Polish Home Army, which represented the Polish government-in-exile, did not try to help the Jews, nor would they give them any weapons, though they themselves were well supplied. When Jewish contacts begged for guns, Home Army representatives said they were saving them for a major action of their own. Finally, they agreed to let the Jews have ten revolvers.

On the third day of battle, the Germans set fire to the ghetto. "Columns of smoke are hanging over the ghetto and are growing larger by the hour," read a communiqué issued that day by the Jewish Fighting Organization. "The force with which the fire is raging is indescribably fierce. . . . Horrible cries and calls for help are heard from the flaming buildings. People enveloped in flames, leap from the windows like live torches." Nevertheless, the resistance continued.

On the fifth day, as the fires raged, German sappers went through the streets, dynamiting one house after another, while German airplanes dropped incendiary bombs.

"This is the eighth day of our life and death struggle," wrote Mordecai Anielewicz on April 27 to his contact outside the ghetto. Anielewicz, twenty-four years old, was the commander of the Jewish Fighting Organization. "It is impossible to describe the conditions under which the Jews in the ghetto are living today. . . . We are nearing our last days, but so long as we have weapons in our hands we shall continue to fight and resist."

On April 28, a message from the Jewish Fighting Organization reached the Polish government-in-exile in London. "On behalf of the millions burnt and murdered and burned alive," it said, "on behalf of those fighting back and all of us condemned to die, we call the whole world: it is imperative that the powerful retaliation of the Allies shall fall upon the bloodthirsty enemy immediately and not in some distant future." But help was not forthcoming.

Heavy fighting within the ghetto continued for thirteen more days and nights. On one day, as a tank made its way down Smocza Street, Jewish fighters pelted it with Molotov cocktails. It burst into flame. "When we saw that the tank was burning we began to dance for joy," wrote Dora Goldkorn. "It was the happiest moment in our lives."

On May 8, the Germans discovered the headquarters of the Jewish Fighting Organization, a large bunker that sheltered 300 noncombatants and was used by the fighters to plan strategy and maintain contact with the outside world. Mordecai Anielewicz was among the fighters when the Germans arrived and surrounded the bunker. They blew up the entrances and then sent gas pouring into the interior. Some of the fighters, including Anielewicz, committed suicide. The rest were overcome by gas. A small number fell near the exists where the fumes were not as strong. They were found later, still alive, by other members of the Jewish Fighting Organization who carried them on their backs on a thirty-hour trek through the sewers of Warsaw to Polish comrades outside the ghetto. Zivia Lubetkin was one of the fighters who escaped to the forest. "Everything was strange," she wrote later. "About us was the green forest, sunlight, a beautiful spring day. It had been a long time since we had known a forest, spring and the sun. All that had been closed up and buried in our frozen hearts for years now trembled, shook and burst and I began to cry. Our future was veiled in darkness and we who had been rescued felt superfluous and alone, abandoned by God and men. What more could be done that we had not done? . . . We lay down on the ground, but could not fall asleep. We thought of the mystery of the world and of man, we remembered the murder of our people, the beloved dead comrades who were part of the ashes of our burned souls. The heart wondered and asked, wondered and asked, but there was no answer."

In the ghetto, the remaining fighters had almost no ammunition left. Iron bars, pieces of furniture, boiling water became their weapons. The Germans sent in tanks and troops with orders to burn, dynamite and destroy the ghetto house by house.

On May 26, General Stroop wrote to his superiors in Berlin. "The former Jewish residential district in Warsaw no longer exists." To celebrate this "great historic victory," the Grand Synagogue on Tlomacka Street, built in 1855, was blown up. The explosion reverberated throughout Warsaw.

On May 27, Yonah Rosen returned to Caesarea with the news Hannah had been waiting for. The rescue mission had been approved. Volunteers were going to be called and interviewed. Yonah had submitted Hannah's name. She could expect to be summoned soon.

"My entire being," she wrote, "is preoccupied with one thing: departure. It's imminent, real. It's possible they'll call me any day now. I imagine various situations and sometimes think about leaving the Land . . . leaving freedom . . . I would like to be able to inhale enough fresh air so as to be able to breathe it even in the Diaspora . . . and to spread it all around me for those who don't know what real freedom is.

"There is absolutely no question but that I must go. The hardships and hazards entailed are quite clear to me. I feel I'll be able to fulfill the assignment. I see everything that has happened to me so far as preparation and training for the mission ahead."

Two days later she wrote again. "I'm waiting to be called. I can't think of anything else. I don't think there is any outer, noticeable change in me. I do my daily work as usual, but sometimes feel as if I'm seeing things from a distance. I look at everything from one point of view only: is it, or is it not necessary for my mission?"

Despite this new perspective, she continued to feel lonely and painfully cut off from other people, though she tried at times to deny it. "I don't want to meet people," she wrote in the same entry. "It'll be easier to leave if I don't." Then she quickly contradicted what she had written. "No," she went on. "That's a lie. Now, more than ever, I'd like someone who is close to me." She ended the entry with strong resolve. "I pray for only one thing: that the period of waiting will not be too long, and that I can see action soon. As for the rest—I'm afraid of nothing. I'm totally self-confident, ready for anything."

In June Hannah was called to Tel Aviv. She was interviewed by representatives of the British Army and representatives of the Haganah. The British were in charge of the interview. In response to a question about what Hannah thought the mission would entail, she calmly recited the priorities she knew the British insisted upon. The first, she said, was to contact local resistance fighters, and with their help, locate captured Allied airmen and help them to escape. The second priority, she said, was to help the Jews. In response to a question about what Hannah would do if she had to choose between saving her mother's life and the lives of twenty British soldiers, Hannah said she knew her mother would forgive her for the choice she would have to make.

Hannah was accepted for the mission. Now her agony began in earnest. Working in the kitchen, in the garden, in the laundry, she waited for word that it was time to go. Yet even now she felt the pain of being an outsider on the kibbutz, unable to join the others, unable not to care.

In September 1943, on the fourth anniversary of her arrival in Palestine, she looked over her years there and blamed herself for having failed to make the connections for which she longed. There was something in her, she believed, or perhaps something missing in her, that kept her alone.

"Am I satisfied?" she wrote. "It's hard to say. I spent two years in Nahalal, after that almost two years at Sdot-Yam and Caesarea. Many struggles, and considerable satisfaction, but always loneliness. No friends, no girl friends, but for Miryam.

"And now I stand before a new assignment again, one that demands great preparation for a difficult and responsible mission. Again a sense of transition coupled with strong emotions, aspirations, tensions. And the everlasting aloneness. Now it's clearer to me than ever that this has nothing to do with outside factors. There's a certain peculiarity within me, and a lack of sociability which keeps me away from people."

Men about whom Hannah could say "only good things" had loved her. But she had not loved them. "All right," she wrote, "at least my heart is far from breaking. But even so, there is something which terrifies me: I am twenty-two years old, and I don't know how to be happy."

She thought of herself as wearing a "placid mask." To the outside world, she was a hard worker, energetic, conscientious, always on the go. But inside where no one could see, she was haunted by the sense of what was missing from her life—love, friendship, the hearty laughter she had once known with George, laughter "about nothing but the joy of living, of being young and alive."

In spite of the terrible circumstances of her days, Hannah blamed herself for her unhappiness. "I have no complaints about life, really," she wrote. "I'm satisfied. I can't imagine a state in which I would be more content. On the contrary. And the assignment which lies ahead draws me on."

In her poems she tried to express the feelings that were too intense even for her diary. This poem, untitled, was written early in the fall.

> You are not alone. Here is your sea.
> The sand, the shore, the sea, the waves,
> The dreams, the hopes that brought you here.
>
> They waited for your coming. They stayed;
> The sand, the shore, the sea, the waves,
> They knew: the black night would bring you here.
>
> And the myriad eyes in the sky
> Wink into your two from on high
> Stealing from the endless sea—a tear.

Yet in spite of her sadness and regret over missed connections, Hannah felt that life made sense now. She had moved to meet needs that were even stronger than the ones she had failed to meet. "In my life's chain of events," she wrote in her diary, "nothing was accidental. Everything happened according to an inner need. I would have been miserable following a road other than the one I chose. . . . I would not have been in harmony with myself."

In December, Hannah received orders to report to Kibbutz Ramat Hakovesh, not far from Tel Aviv, for the first part of her training. She did not write about this in her diary, but while in Tel Aviv, where she was to board the bus, she visited Miryam and gave her a letter to be delivered to George if he should arrive in the Land while Hannah was gone. Miryam agreed not to ask any questions about the letter or about Hannah's mission, which was classified a military secret. Hannah had told members of Kibbutz Sdot-Yam just that she was reporting to the Palmach for basic training, which was partially true. Basic training was the first phase of Hannah's training. Parachute training was second. Later, in Egypt, she would be taught the skills of the saboteur, the infiltrator and the spy.

In all, 240 youths had been accepted for the mission; thirty-two were being trained for the Balkans. In addition to Hannah, two others were women: Chaviva Reik and Sarah Braverman. Volunteers were trained in shifts. At Ramat Hakovesh, mission members were taught unarmed fighting, mostly based on judo, and armed fighting, using basic weapons (like the knife and the club) as well as more sophisticated weapons (the sten gun, tommy gun, German schmeisser and the .45 Colt automatic). They also learned to disassemble and assemble the weapons, quickly, silently and blindfolded.

From Ramat Hakovesh, Hannah returned briefly to her kibbutz, then she was back in Tel Aviv to board a bus to Ramat David, a kibbutz near Nahalal that housed the Middle East Training Center for Parachutists. While in Tel Aviv, Hannah tried to arrange immigration papers for her mother.

At Ramat David, she amazed everyone by her fearlessness in learning to parachute jump. "It's nothing," she said later to a new volunteer named Yoel Palgi. "You go up in a plane, you jump, and you're right back on the ground. I'll never forget how Nahalal looked from the air. It was a great experience. You'll love it." "She spoke as naturally and plainly as if she were describing what she had had for breakfast that morning," Yoel wrote later.

Back at Caesarea to await orders for the third phase of her training, Hannah took walks on the beach, swam in the sea, worked and waited. In mid-January, she received orders to return to Tel Aviv. From there, members of the mission would depart together for Cairo and the final part of their training.

"We were all tense at the thought of leaving Eretz," Yoel Palgi wrote. "None dared admit to the other how difficult it was to leave; everyone wondered whether he would ever see the Land again. We were all parting from our dear ones, our settlements, our land. It was a silent parting, one that neither relieved tensions nor lightened spirits. We had to avoid arousing curiosity and questions. The mission itself was a silent one; no one must know we were going armed with a sling to do battle with the powerful enemy."

During this waiting period Hannah and Yoel often went out and "at such times," Yoel later wrote, "we would try to divert our minds from the mission that lay ahead, but of course it was difficult. Hannah's face would occasionally turn sad. Once she told me that her mother was still living in Budapest, alone, and that she was supposed to come to Eretz. She was frightened her mother would arrive when we were who knows where and that there would be no one to meet her. She also told me about her brother who was due to arrive any day, and probably would—straight after our departure. She said she had written him a letter in which she tried to tell him about the Land and guide his first steps."

Hannah imagined George's arrival in a poem she had written the previous year.

> If you came suddenly from across the street—
> Hands in your pockets, laughter in your eyes,
> And footsteps sounding with a familiar beat—
> I would stand still in sudden shock and fright
> To see that wonderful, that precious sight.
>
> Until your image would pierce me in depth
> The fires of doubt within myself I smother
> Opening my arms in wing-flight to embrace you
> Half-laughing, half-crying: Brother!

The day Hannah's group was to leave for Egypt, Hannah got a message she could hardly believe: George was in Haifa. He had arrived on an immigrant ship called the *Nyassa* and had been interned in Atlit, a British-run camp for illegal immigrants. He had managed to persuade one of the British soldiers to search Hannah out and tell her of his arrival. Yoel Palgi was with Hannah when she got the news. "I hardly recognized in her the

Just before she departed for Egypt, Hannah met her brother George for what was to be the last time.

strong self-assured young woman I had come to know so well," he wrote. "Tears flowed from her eyes. With difficulty I managed to obtain bus tickets for Haifa, and accompanied her there ..." Yoel also contacted their superiors and was able to have their departure for Egypt put off until the next day.

Hannah took back from Miryam the letter she had written in December and sent a telegram to her mother telling her George had arrived at last. At the Atlit camp, as an officer in the British Army, Hannah was able to make her way through the red tape and get permission for George to leave the compound for a few hours. Brother and sister walked out under the brooding late afternoon sky. Hannah could hardly believe that George had arrived at last. George could hardly believe that Hannah was going away. He told her part of the incredible story of his escape from Europe, how he had made his way from France to Spain, where he spent over a month in various prisons, passed himself off as a French-Canadian, and finally managed to board an immigrant ship that made its way through the British patrols to Palestine.

Hannah could tell George almost nothing of what she was doing, where she was going, when she would be back. She told him only that she was a radio officer, and she gave him the letter she had retrieved from Miryam.

Darling George!

Sometimes one writes letters one does not intend sending. Letters one must write without asking oneself, "I wonder whether this will ever reach its destination."

Day after tomorrow I am starting something new. Perhaps it's madness. Perhaps it's fantastic. Perhaps it is dangerous. Perhaps one in a hundred—or one in a thousand—pays with his life. Perhaps with less than his life, perhaps with more. Don't ask questions. You'll eventually know what it's about.

George, I must explain something to you. I must exonerate myself. I must prepare myself for that moment when you arrive inside the frontiers of the Land, waiting for that moment when, after six years, we will meet again, and you will ask, "Where is she?" and they'll abruptly answer, "She's not here."

I wonder, will you understand? I wonder, will you believe that it is more than a childish wish for adventure, more than youthful romanticism that attracted me? I wonder, will you feel that I could not do otherwise, that this was something I had to do?

There are events without which one's life becomes unimportant, a worthless toy; and there are times when one is commanded to do something, even at the price of one's life.

I'm afraid, George, that feelings turn into empty phrases even though they are so impassioned before they turn into words. I don't know whether you'll sense the doubts, the conflicts, and after every struggle the renewed decision.

It is difficult because I am alone. If I had someone with whom I could talk freely, uninhibitedly—if only the entire burden were not mine, if only I could talk to you. If there is anyone who would understand me, I think you would be that one. But who knows . . . six years is a long time.

But enough about myself. Perhaps I have already said too much. I would like to tell you a few things about the new life, the new home, as I see them. I don't want to influence you. You'll see for yourself what the country is. But I want to tell you how I see it.

First of all—I love it. I love its hundred faces, its hundred climates, its many-faceted life. I love the old and the new in it; I love it because it is ours. No, not ours, but because we can make ourselves believe it is ours.

And I respect it. Not everything. I respect the people who believe in something, respect their idealistic struggle with the daily realities. I respect those who don't live just for the moment, or for money. And I think there are more such people here than anywhere else on earth. And finally, I think that this is the only solution for us, and for this reason I don't doubt its future, though I think it will be very difficult and combative.

As far as the kibbutz is concerned, I don't think it is perfect, and it will probably pass through many phases. But in today's circumstances it best suits our aims, and is the closest to our concept of a way of life—about this I have absolutely no doubt.

We have need of one thing: people who are brave and without prejudices, who are not robots, who want to think for themselves and not accept outmoded ideas. It is easy to place laws in the hands of man, to tell him to live by them. It is more difficult to follow those laws. But most difficult of all is to impose laws upon oneself, while being constantly self-analytical and self-vigilant. I think this is the highest form of law enforcement, and at the same time the only just form. And this form of law can only build a new, contented life.

I often ask myself what the fate of the kibbutz will be when the magic and novelty of construction and creation wear off, when the struggle for existence assumes reality and—

according to plan—becomes an organized, abundant communal life. What will the incentive of the people be, what will fill their lives? I don't know the answer. But that day is so far in the future that it is best to think of existing matters.

Don't think I see everything through rose-colored glasses. My faith is a subjective matter, and not the result of outer conditions. I see the difficulties clearly, both inside and out. But I see the good side, and above all, as I said before, I think this is the only way.

I did not write about something that constantly preoccupies my thoughts: Mother. I can't.

Enough of this letter. I hope you will never receive it. But if you do, only after we have met.

And if it should be otherwise, George dear, I embrace you with everlasting love.

Your sister.

P.S. I wrote the letter at the beginning of the parachute training course.

Hannah took the letter back after George had read it. She told him she couldn't answer any questions about it and he did not ask. Then it was time for him to return to Atlit and for Hannah to return to Tel Aviv. The next day, she was gone.

PART TWO

1944

CHAPTER 9

JANUARY

"I leave happily and of my own free will, with full knowledge of the difficulties ahead"

THE car ride to Cairo took ten hours. "The drive was pleasant since I came with a group of good-natured people," Hannah wrote to George almost as soon as she arrived. "We sang, talked, and even slept . . . I had plenty of time to think, and thus naturally thought about you. Again and again I thanked Providence that we could at least meet, even though only for such a very short time."

Later, Yoel Palgi wrote that they had all "felt the seriousness" of their departure from the Land. He thought that Hannah, who had had to leave the brother for whom she had waited so long, had reason to be most distressed. "But she said nothing as we sang, joked and planned all kinds of projects for after our return," he recalled. "We decided that at the end of the war we would return in a big bomber, and each of us would parachute into his own settlement."

There were five mission members in the car, plus two British drivers. "We were soldiers, arrogant," Palgi recalled, "and ill mannered, and we failed to take the Britishers' feelings into account." Hannah, however, remembered, speaking English with them and translating the others' jokes "so they could laugh with us, understand our silly plans, feel involved, one of us."

After they crossed the border and were officially in Egypt, Hannah "declared suddenly" that she wanted to learn to drive! "We protested vigorously," Palgi wrote, "saying she would endanger our lives. But she insisted that it was as good a time as any to learn. She slid behind the wheel, listened as one of the drivers explained what was what, and began driving."

For a few hundred yards, Hannah drove slowly, with painstaking care and attention. Then, apparently sure of herself, she accelerated. The others begged her to drive more slowly, but she "sped on furiously through the desert." Palgi himself, "expecting the worst," closed his eyes whenever another car approached. But Hannah handled the car smoothly, with complete assurance. Finally they all relaxed. "She drove for hours on end, without tiring," Palgi wrote later, and didn't hand the wheel back to the driver until they had reached the Suez Canal.

In Cairo, all thirty-two crew members were quartered in private homes. They attended meetings and workshops and developed their own strategies and plans in detail. Experts from the countries to which they were heading attended their meetings and gave them advice. One of them was a young Yugoslavian named Reuven Dafne.

Reuven had met Hannah earlier, when he was asked to give a briefing in Tel Aviv. "During my sessions with the group," he wrote about that meeting, "a girl—the only girl in it—attracted my attention by her alert participation throughout the long discussions of the problems involved in the execution of the daring plan. At first it didn't occur to me that she was also an emissary. I thought she, too, had been called in to give information concerning one of the countries the mission was heading for. When I realized she was actually one of the group I began talking to her, and was enormously impressed by her great fervor."

Now in Cairo, Reuven and Hannah met again. Hannah implored him to join the group himself, emphasizing that "the participation of someone who was completely at home in Yugo-slavia would make things much easier for the group assigned to that area." Partly because of Hannah's urging, Reuven did join. As the two of them worked together, he was more impressed with Hannah than ever, though he came to be somewhat baffled by her intensity and passion. On a trip to the Auxiliary Transport Services Unit, for example, Reuven recalled that Hannah was "happy, cheerful, joked with all of us, including our Arab driver, yet didn't take her mind off the mission, making suggestions and planning details for action." He noticed that she was very intense and quickly changed from one mood to another. "One moment she would be rolling with laughter, the next aflame with the fervor of the mission," Reuven wrote. "I felt that a kind of divine spark must be burning in the depths of her being, motivating her."

Hannah and the other members of her crew expected to leave for Europe within a week of their arrival in Cairo in late January. But their departure was delayed from day to day, and then from week to week. There were rumors that Rumania and Hungary were on the point of collapse, which made the young volunteers even more anxious to get underway—to get there, if possible, before the Germans did. "But this was of no concern to the Allies," Palgi complained. "What was a matter of conscience to us was, to them, a routine matter. We knew our lives and the lives of our people hung in the balance, and that the British were certainly attempting to protect us as individuals. But in so doing they were preventing us from helping our people, and naturally there were endless arguments, even serious clashes between our British sponsors and ourselves."

Hannah, Palgi reported, was the chief rebel. "And she was not always right. On the contrary. More often than not, she was wrong. At the time I could not even distinguish between her tense impatience and her dedication to the mission," he wrote. Her indifference to personal safety and refusal to even discuss anything that might delay the mission made him begin to wonder whether he would be able to work with her once they were in enemy territory. "She didn't appear to be sufficiently cooperative," he wrote, alluding to Hannah's intolerance and argumentativeness. "She was totally lacking in caution, and refused to accept discipline. She insisted that we divide up the fields of activity in advance, so we would not have to waste time on such matters once we were dropped. She wanted to be sure she got her share of the action, that she would not be left out."

To pass the time, the young paratroopers in Hannah's crew wandered about Cairo and toured the countryside, but it was impossible for any of them to generate much enthusiasm for sightseeing. "Today I went on an excursion again," Hannah wrote to George in February. "This time to the royal graves of Luxor. They are interesting, monumental creations. But as a matter of fact I don't have the patience for such things now. As far as I can see, we're moving on next week, and I am tensely awaiting the new assignment."

They did not leave the next week, however, or the week after that. No explanation for the delay was given. To crew members' questions about when they would depart, there was only one answer: soon.

"The only fortunate thing," Hannah wrote in another letter at the end of February, "is that there are so many soldiers here from Ma'agan, and that one by one they take trips home so I can send you a letter, and along with this one a little gift. I would like to send you every nice thing I see, to make up for the many years I could send nothing."

On or about the first of March, British Intelligence learned that the Germans were preparing to occupy Hungary. Since this would probably happen in a matter of days, the Hungarian crew was told that their plans would have to be changed: they could not be dropped into Hungary now. All the crew members— Yonah Rosen, Abba Berdichev, Reuven Dafne, Yoel Palgi, Peretz Goldstein, and Hannah—protested. They wanted to leave for Hungary at once, and arrive before the Germans, but they were overruled. They were informed they would have to wait at least a week, while more information was gathered; then they would be dropped into Yugoslavia. There they would rendezvous with the partisans, and at the right time, if they could, they would make their way into Hungary. The British would not consider any alternatives.

On March 10, the crew was told to get ready. They were going to be flown to Bari, Italy, a major port and a center of Allied military activity. From there they would make arrangements for the flight to Yugoslavia. "I leave happily and of my own free will, with full knowledge of the difficulties ahead," Hannah wrote to the secretary of her kibbutz in her last letter from Cairo. "I consider my mission a privilege, and at the same time a duty."

The crew left Cairo under the guidance of forty-two-year-old Enzo Sereni, a native of Italy and the scion of a highly distinguished family, who had volunteered to help the mission and who later parachuted behind enemy lines in northern Italy himself. "Sereni breathed more easily in his native land, felt free and stimulated," Reuven recalled. "He chatted with everyone he met, played with the children." To Reuven's surprise, though Enzo and Hannah clearly liked one another and sought each other's company, they argued intensely time and again. On the day of their arrival in Italy, for example, they argued about the Italian people, Enzo explaining and forgiving their role in the war, Hannah condemning.

The next day, on the way to Brindisi to make final preparations for the trip to Yugoslavia, the two argued again, this time about the existence of God. "Enzo was an extremely astute man of great experience, a student of philosophy, and he fervently postulated God's existence. Opposing him with clear, penetrating logic was twenty-two-year-old Hannah." Observing Hannah's "forcefulness, determination and passion," Reuven, like Yoel, began to wonder whether he "would be able to work with her. . . . I was convinced it would not be easy . . . that she would be difficult to sway from her stand once her mind was made up about something. Eventually I became positive this was so, and frequently we exchanged heated words."

But Hannah's passion was her strength too, Reuven noted, and because of it she was able to help the others. "Never once did she allow us to become dispirited or discouraged," he wrote. "She would explain with iron logic how we could extricate ourselves from any predicament, and her inner conviction would reassure us." Though Hannah herself was sometimes discouraged too, "renewed strength constantly welled from the depths of her being."

On the night of March 13, Reuven, Yonah Rosen, Abba Berdichev and Hannah were told to get ready to leave for the Brindisi airport. They would take off for Yugoslavia that night. Yoel Palgi and Peretz Goldstein would follow later. Hannah was overjoyed. "She sang the whole way back to the village where we were quartered," Reuven wrote, "and made us sing along with her." Reuven himself, who had just learned that his father and older brother were in a concentration camp, could not bring himself to join them. "Again it was Hannah who understood," he wrote, "—and how well she understood—my feelings, and tried to prop up my spirits and comfort me."

At the airport, the crew members met the officer in charge of their operation. "Despite his British reserve he couldn't restrain his surprise at seeing a woman among us," Reuven recalled. "The British boys working in the large parachute storeroom where we were taken to put on our harnesses couldn't take their eyes off Hannah, nor hide their amazement." Hannah never referred to the stir she caused and seems to have taken it all in stride. A group of American paratroopers, as surprised as the British to see a woman in the military hangar, assumed that Hannah was a paratrooper's wife who had come to see him off. "When they met us again, just before we took off," Reuven wrote, "they were shocked to see her and one of them, extremely moved, walked over to her and wordlessly shook her hand." Hannah didn't seem to understand the handshake, but smiled and nodded in a comradely way. "Her charming and simple reaction threw the astounded American completely off balance."

At a few minutes past midnight on the fourteenth of March,

a clear moonlit night, the mission to Hungary took off. Hannah's face was aglow. "She exuded happiness and excitement," Reuven recalled. As far as anyone knew, Hungary had not yet been occupied. Perhaps they would still be able to get there before the Germans.

On March 15, 1944, the Regent of Hungary, Miklos Horthy, was summoned to Klessheim Castle, Hitler's headquarters, in Germany. There he was kept under house arrest while Hitler berated him and the government he headed for their treachery to Germany. In fact, Hungary *had* been a poor ally, motivated more by a desire to regain lost territory than by a desire to conquer the world or destroy its Jews. Its loyalty to Germany and its support of the war had zigzagged from the beginning. By February 1943, when the Russian Army defeated the German Army at Stalingrad, and began to push the Germans back across central Europe, the Hungarian government had grown more and more anxious to break its ties to Germany and ease its way out of the war. In April 1943, Hitler had summoned Horthy to Germany and charged him and his government with failing to fulfill their obligations to Germany. But the Horthy government had continued its attempts to disengage itself from the war. In May, Horthy's Prime Minister, Miklos Kallay, had publicly defied Hitler's order to deport the Jews of Hungary to Poland, saying that the Hungarian government would not agree to the "resettlement" of its Jews as long as the Germans did not explain exactly where they were being resettled. In August, Kallay had broadcast an appeal for peace, and in February 1944, Hitler learned that Kallay was trying to set up a secret conference with the Allies. In March the German leader decided to tighten his grip on his lukewarm ally and to do something about the Hungarian Jews while he still could.

By March 19, when Horthy was allowed to return to Budapest, German officials were in charge of every government office and agency. Liberal politicians and other Hungarians opposed to

German soldiers on the Fisherman's Bastion in Budapest. Hitler ordered the Nazi takeover while he kept Horthy with him in Germany.

fascism had been arrested. A German military task force was in control of the Budapest airport, and German military personnel and police could be seen throughout the city. Arriving in Budapest on the same day as Horthy was German Minister of the Reich and General Plenipotentiary Edmund Veesenmayer. His job was to coordinate the German personnel now in Hungary and to supervise the Hungarian government itself. The next day, Adolph Eichmann, Germany's "expert in Jewish affairs" arrived, and a few days later, his band of "deportation specialists," the Eichmann Special Commando Unit. They were, as historian Nora Levin put it, "the most devastating unit of Jewish killing specialists in the history of the Holocaust."

Eichmann set up his offices in the Majestic, a complex of luxurious apartment suites set on a hillside overlooking Budapest. From there he devised the strategies and set up the apparatus for killing the Jews of Hungary. He did this so swiftly that his work in other countries seems sluggish in comparison. The Jews in the outer provinces were to be rounded up first. The roundups would be completely secret, so the Jews in the inner provinces would not have a chance to flee. When the Jews in the first roundups were on their way to the death camps in Poland, the Commando Unit would move on to the central provinces. Finally, they would round up the Jews in Budapest itself. As the plan went into operation, Eichmann made personal assurances to the leaders of the Jewish community in Budapest. The Jews of Hungary had nothing to fear, he told them, if only they cooperated.

"I am not an advocate of violence," he said to a gathering of Jewish leaders in his suite at the Majestic, "because I value manpower. But any opposition will be broken. If you think of joining the partisans or employing their methods, I shall have you mercilessly slaughtered." Then he went on comfortingly. "After the war the Jews will be free. All the Jewish measures will be abandoned and the Germans will again be good-natured as before." Eichmann admitted that in other countries Jews had been killed, but he said that in Hungary, they would not be. Even individual acts of violence against them would not be tolerated. "You tell me if anyone harms you and I will protect you," he promised. "You can trust me and talk freely to me—as I am quite frank with you."

The roundups and deportations from the provinces proceeded without a hitch. In no other country were so many Jews taken into the death machine so fast. Although the cloak of secrecy was never entirely penetrated, some reports of gruesome conditions in provincial ghettoes and camps, where Jews were kept while waiting for trains to Poland, reached the Jewish leaders in Budapest. They appealed to Eichmann, who promptly reassured them. "Not a single word of the reports is true," he said, "for as I have just inspected the provincial ghettoes, I really ought to know. The accommodations of the Jews is no worse than that of the German soldiers during maneuvers and fresh air will only do their health the world of good."

CHAPTER 10

JUNE 9

"It was as if the earth beneath her were on fire"

"I jumped," Reuven wrote, recalling the night the crew parachuted into Yugoslavia, "and she [Hannah] was right behind me. A few moments later we were on the soil of Yugoslavia, land of the partisans."

A partisan is a guerrilla fighter, a member of an unofficial, independent group fighting an enemy on territory that the enemy controls. In Europe, partisans arose in most of the countries conquered by the Nazis. Hiding by day and striking at night, they harrassed the Germans and committed acts of sabotage against supply depots, train lines, military camps, field headquarters—wherever they thought they could hurt or weaken the Germans' hold or slow down their progress. There were partisans even in cities like Paris, but most partisan units operated in the country-side. They lived in makeshift encampments in the forests, ate what they could forage or steal or what they were given by sympathetic local farmers. For weapons, they had whatever they could find, steal or capture from the enemy—though as the war

A group of Jewish partisans somewhere in Eastern Europe.

progressed, most units also received aid from the Allied countries.

In Yugoslavia, partisans appeared in the spring of 1941, almost as soon as the German invasion was over. The reprisals they faced were horrifying—in some places, the Germans killed one hundred civilians for every German soldier the partisans killed, wounded fifty civilians for every soldier the partisans wounded. Even so, by 1944 the partisans virtually controlled the mountains. They were aided and kept in supplies primarily by the British, who had become their main support and with whom they often worked. It was the British who arranged for a partisan unit to meet the paratroopers from Palestine, and it was as British Army officers that Reuven, Hannah and the others were greeted—their true identities and real mission a secret from everyone. It was in partisan headquarters a few days after they landed that Reuven and Hannah heard the radio report: Hungary had just been taken over by the Germans.

"It was the first time I saw Hannah cry," Reuven wrote. "I thought she was crying solely because of her mother, whom I knew she adored, and to whom certainly anything could happen now. But amidst her sobs she exclaimed, 'What will happen to all of them . . . to the million Jews in Hungary? They're in German hands now—and we're sitting here . . . just sitting.' "

Hannah wanted to proceed to the border without delay, but that could not be done. The Germans had just launched a major offensive and recaptured the stretch of borderland where the paratroopers were to have crossed into Hungary. Now they would have to join another partisan unit, 200 miles away, which controlled a different stretch of borderland. Hannah found this situation almost intolerable.

"Her conscience knew no rest," Reuven wrote. "It was as if the earth beneath her were on fire." But though she pored over maps, brooded and argued, the crossing into Hungary was delayed.

"For months we wandered across that land together," Reuven wrote, "witnessing the cruel yet wonderful, ferocious partisan battle for victory and liberty. We saw incredible heroism and we saw destruction—entire towns and villages in total ruin, flames consuming the labor of generations."

As they traveled, Reuven worked on ways to help Allied prisoners of war and captured airmen to escape the Germans and reach partisan territory. He plotted maps, sent out information by radio, set up search parties for stranded aviators. The Germans put a price on his head. Britain decorated him for exceptional gallantry.

Wherever they went, Reuven recalled, people were drawn to Hannah, "the young British officer smart in her army uniform, pistol strapped to her waist. . . . she became something of a legend." It wasn't only because she was a woman that people noticed her. Women fought alongside men in almost every partisan unit in Yugoslavia and the rest of Europe. Instead, "there was a special, mysterious quality about Hannah which excited [people's] wonder and respect," Reuven wrote. "She fascinated them."

One evening, Reuven, Hannah and two other members of the group were invited to a partisan festival high in the mountains. Fully armed women and men thronged the streets and filled the town hall. When the young paratroopers entered, the crowd cheered them as representatives of the British Empire. "We felt sad," Reuven wrote later, "that we had to keep our true identities secret, that we could not share with them the full purpose of our mission."

One of the commanders asked Hannah to come forward and speak to the people. Reuven acted as her interpreter. "Her every sentence was greeted by the crowd with appreciative, cheerful enthusiasm," he wrote. Afterward, the people formed circles and danced. It was "wildly exhilarating" to watch them—rifles strapped to their shoulders, hand grenades swinging from their belts in rhythm with the music. As Reuven watched, Hannah joined the main circle and danced for hours.

But in contrast to those "happy hours of relaxation," Reuven wrote, "there were cruel, fearsome endless days under fire, facing death." Once they trekked for forty-eight consecutive hours without rest, without food, through forests riddled with German patrols. Yoel Palgi, who arrived in Yugoslavia about a month later than the others, thought that the hardships and dangers they faced had made them stronger and more resilient than any of them would have thought possible. Hannah in particular seemed fired by a new sense of her own power. It was as if before this time, she had been only vaguely aware of "the forces that lay dormant within her," Yoel wrote. "Now she was fully conscious of them and had unlimited faith in herself."

She had changed in other ways too, Yoel wrote. She seemed "cold" and "sharp," he wrote, her reasoning "razor-edged." She "no longer trusted strangers," and "her eyes no longer sparkled." Yoel had found Hannah difficult to get along with before, but "she was ten times more so now"—she was impatient, stubborn, unwilling to listen to suggestions or "reasonable" advice. She objected bitterly to the long stay in Yugoslavia and thought they should take matters into their own hands at once. The other crew members maintained their respect for the chain of command and for discipline. Hannah felt that the moral obligation to help was more important than anything else. "We don't have the right to think of our own safety," she said to Yoel. "We are the only ones who can possibly help . . . we don't have the right to hesitate. Even if the chances of our success are miniscule, we must go." So passionately convinced was Hannah that "it was impossible to oppose her," Yoel wrote. "She turned against anyone who disagreed with her point of view."

Hannah no longer kept a diary, but her feelings—her love, her compassion, her longing to help, the dreams and visions that made her so unyielding—are clear in the poem she called "We Gather Flowers." She wrote it in Hebrew while traveling with the partisans.

> We gathered flowers in the fields and mountains,
> We breathed the fresh winds of spring,
> We were drenched with the warmth of the sun's rays
> In our Homeland, in our beloved home.
>
> We go out to our brothers in exile,
> To the suffering of winter, to frost in the night.
> Our hearts will bring tidings of springtime
> Our lips sing the song of light.

Though everyone disagreed with Hannah's ideas about what the mission should do, when they were in the field and in danger, she was unmistakably their leader. Her passion and single-mindedness—the very things that made her so difficult to talk to—made her judgment under fire sharp and clear, her decisions quick and appropriate. Though she wouldn't accept discipline from others, her self-discipline was unparalleled. "Thanks to Hannah," Yoel wrote, "we learned to control our desire for revenge when confronting the enemy. . . . She always said, 'That's not what we came for. We must save ourselves for our mission, not place our lives in jeopardy.' And we always bowed to her wisdom."

Reuven recalled an occasion when he, Hannah and two others were alone in the forest, cut off from the partisans by a German raiding party. "Our nerves were at breaking point,"

Reuven wrote. "There were moments when we thought we would be unable to hold out another instant, but we plodded on, praying for a miracle. At the edge of the forest the Germans, shooting wildly in all directions, were so close they could have stepped on us—but miraculously they missed us. I'll never forget Hannah's amazing composure. I would glance at her from time to time, lying there, pistol cocked, a heavenly radiance on her face. I was overwhelmed by wonder for this unique girl."

On another occasion Reuven and Hannah were in a tiny village friendly to the partisans when the Germans launched a surprise attack. "A hail of bullets suddenly burst upon the village," Reuven wrote. "The partisans had to retreat, seeking shelter wherever possible, and the majority escaped. The villagers ran about in total confusion, sliding down the hillside or sheltering under rocks. We were completely alone, cut off, surrounded by the enemy. We slid down a rope, continued running in an open valley, entirely exposed to the firing from the encircling hills. We tried desperately to catch up with the retreating partisans. All around we heard cries of fear from clusters of bewildered civilians who stumbled along, clutching pathetic belongings, their children . . . The cries of the wounded and the groans of the dying filled the stillness; people dropped like wounded birds. All about us there was horrible panic."

Reuven and Hannah made it to the forest, where they fell to the ground exhausted. For a while they lay silently in the bushes, clutching their rifles, looking about, "listening to the incessant tattoo of bullets, the moaning of the wounded. Suddenly, a group of German soldiers came into view and my finger tightened on the trigger," Reuven recalled. "But Hannah, calm, in control of her senses, stopped me. Firmly, quietly, she said, 'Stop! Don't shoot!' Her eyes reminded me of that which I had forgotten in all the chaos: our goal was to rescue our brothers; shooting at the enemy could only endanger our mission."

One evening, Reuven and Hannah made their way to a village that was under the command of a partisan they hadn't yet met. They had been at headquarters for about an hour when the commander arrived. "I was astounded," Reuven wrote. "I knew her! We had been childhood friends, had lived in the same district, had played together in the streets of the capital." The woman was only in her early twenties, but "the years of terror had left their mark on her face," Reuven wrote, "and despite her youth her hair was streaked with gray."

The woman had thought the paratroopers, who were well-known among the partisans by that time, were members of the British Army in Yugoslavia on a military mission of some kind. She was shocked to learn that they were all Jewish and that they had come from Palestine. In the course of their conversation, it turned out that all the partisans in the room at that moment were Jewish too. Moved beyond words, they felt united by a "sacred bond," Reuven wrote. The Palestinians told the Yugoslavian Jews about the Homeland they had been working to build. The Yugoslavians revealed to them "who had been so protected in Palestine from reality" the "horrible suffering" of the Jews of Europe—the grisly roundups and murders of hundreds of thousands of defenseless people, babies and children, women and men. Hannah spoke very little, and Reuven could see that she was deeply shaken. Just before she crossed the Hungarian border, she handed him a piece of paper on which she had written the four-line poem that, Reuven noted, "revealed the passion within her."

BLESSED IS THE MATCH

Blessed is the match consumed
in kindling flame.

Blessed is the flame that burns
in the secret fastness of the heart.

Blessed is the heart with strength to stop
its beating for honor's sake.

Blessed is the match consumed
in kindling flame.

Hannah's restlessness now turned into resistance. She would wait no longer. If the crew did not receive instructions to enter Hungary, she would go without instructions. If no one would go with her, she would go alone.

On May 13, Hannah and Yoel made their way to a landing field high in the mountains where the partisans were expecting a supply drop. They trudged through the mud, discussing "this and that"—Hannah telling Yoel "the secrets of the poultry trade," the two of them debating political issues in the Land. "It was a cold, clear night," Yoel recalled. "The partisans had made a bonfire and were sitting round it. They began singing, and the wild song penetrated the silence, the voices bewailing the anguish of an oppressed people. That night we liked the partisans very much . . . they had learned the truest, most profound lesson a nation can learn: the need to live as free men, and to be willing to sacrifice their lives for liberty. . . . We sat with them, warmed ourselves at their fire, tried to sing along with them."

Suddenly, Hannah got up and asked Yoel to walk with her. "As we walked side by side in the still dark night, she poured out her heart, saying many of the things she had said before, only that night she spoke differently. It was not the cold, logical woman talking, the stubborn young officer . . . but a sensitive young woman, perceptive and tender. She said she was overwhelmed by inner turmoil and struggle, that although she was aware she was not always sensible, ours was not a sensible reasonable time, that she felt incapable of waiting on the sidelines while thousands were being slaughtered."

"It's better to die and free our conscience," she said to Yoel, "than to return with the knowledge we didn't even try. Each of us is free to act as he thinks best, and I quite understand the way the rest of you feel about discipline. But for me this is not a question that can be decided by authority."

As Hannah spoke, Yoel realized that she was speaking for him too. It was time to cross the border, with or without orders. They decided to go separately, because of the great danger involved, and to try to meet again in Budapest. They would look for each other every Saturday in front of the Great Synagogue after Sabbath services, in front of the Cathedral if Jewish services were no longer being held. "She was happy," Yoel wrote, ". . . and began describing to me the things she had imagined, the things she hoped would happen. She drew imaginary portraits of Jewish partisans sitting around campfires, singing songs of Eretz, the forests of Europe echoing the sad songs of Jewish freedom fighters." They parted as "dear, close friends."

The next morning, Hannah went off with a group of partisans heading for a Yugoslav village forty miles to the south—as close to the Hungarian border as they would take her. Reuven, who did not plan to cross the border at that time, decided to go with them as far as the village. The trip took twenty-six days because they had to circle and backtrack around German patrols combing the forests. Sometimes they slept in stables; sometimes they hid during the day and traveled only at night.

On June 6, as the little band maneuvered through the mountains of Yugoslavia, the mightiest striking force in the history of warfare—150,000 British, Canadian and American soldiers, 1,500 tanks, 2,727 ships and small water craft, and 1,200 airplanes—crossed the English Channel and began the invasion of German-occupied France. Three days later, 1,000 miles away, Hannah and the group of partisans reached the border village that had been their destination. There, sheltered by the partisans, was a group of refugees who had just escaped from Hungary. Among them were three men who were willing to return with Hannah: Kallos and Fleischmann, from the Jewish underground, and Jacques Tissandier, an escaped French prisoner of war. Reuven listened as the four worked out the plans for their journey. He grew more and more uncomfortable but found it "quite impossible" to talk about his reservations with Hannah. "She absolutely refused to wait another day, another hour, and all my efforts to persuade her to wait a trifle longer were in vain. She had firmly decided to cross over without further delay—if necessary even without an escort. That was that. The matter was settled."

The partisans agreed to take Hannah, Kallos, Fleischmann and Jacques to the edge of the forested border area. They would leave as soon as it was dark. Hannah was in very high spirits. She joked with everyone, Reuven recalled, and she laughed easily, but "beneath the banter there was a sharp edge to her jesting, a steady note of earnestness."

That evening they had an early supper, and as soon as it was finished, Hannah asked Reuven to go outside with her. Walking through the yard to the orchard, they discussed ways in which to find one another if and when Reuven too should make his way to Budapest. Hannah was relaxed and confident, and seemed eager to get going. But she was well aware of the risks she would be taking, and as they walked along, she asked Reuven for a pellet of cyanide—the deadly poison that was standard equipment for anyone going behind enemy lines, to be used if and when suicide seemed the best option. Reuven refused. He thought that if he gave her the cyanide, he would undermine her confidence. He wanted above all to encourage her, and "remove all doubts of her success." Hannah let the matter drop.

It was seven o'clock and dusk had fallen when the head of the partisan unit came to tell Hannah that they would be leaving in fifteen minutes. "Hannah was extraordinarily cheerful during those last minutes," Reuven wrote. She was "radiant, the epitome of a free soul." Returning to the house for her gear, she joked with Reuven, reminded him of some of the funny things that had happened to them in Yugoslavia, and at the same time seemed totally calm and relaxed, alert, and self-assured. "She was bubbling with joy, forthright, impish, and amazingly carefree. She seemed like someone about to embark upon an experience she had been looking forward to for years." She spoke about the day the war would be over and they would all meet again in the Land. "We'll rent a big bus," she said, "and drive up and down the country. First we'll visit all the settlements that sent members on this mission. Then we'll arrange celebrations in those settlements, and we'll tell them everything that happened to us, and we'll spin tall tales. In addition, we'll visit the entire country, from Dan to Be'er Sheva. We'll spend the month traveling."

Reuven and Hannah left the house together. In case anyone from the village was watching, they walked for a while in the direction leading away from the border. Then they stopped and Hannah held out her hand. "Till we meet again," she said, "soon, I hope, in enemy territory." Reuven watched as Hannah turned and walked quickly away to join the others. At the bend in the road she stopped and waved farewell. It was almost dark, the ninth of June, 1944.

"I didn't know," Reuven wrote, "I would never see her again."

CHAPTER 11

JUNE 17

"The...bruises on her face were like knife wounds in my own flesh"

"I waited in vain for her at the Synagogue," Yoel Palgi wrote years later. "I looked for her at the Cathedral." But Hannah did not keep their rendezvous in Budapest. With Kallos, Fleischmann and Jacques Tissandier, she had made her way only as far as the Hungarian village of Mureska Sobatica, a long journey still from the capital city. Before then they had hiked for days through the thick forests of eastern Hungary, a compass and rough map their only guides. They crossed and recrossed the winding, turbulent River Drava, swimming with one hand, holding parts of Hannah's disassembled radio-transmitter with the other. They were not sure how far they had come, or whether they were still on course, when they reached the outskirts of a village. Kallos and Fleischmann decided to scout it. If it was Mureska Sobatica, they were on course. They might also be able to find contacts there, members of the Jewish underground who would help them get false identity papers and travel permits. Hannah and Jacques agreed to wait in the woods, with the transmitter, until Kallos and Fleischmann returned.

But Kallos and Fleischmann did not return. While on their way to the village, they were stopped by two Hungarian police officers. According to Fleischmann, the officers asked them only routine questions about where they were going and seemed ready to release them—when suddenly, Kallos panicked. "What took place in the mind of one of the boys [Kallos] we'll never know," Palgi wrote later. "What we do know is that instead of trying to bluff his way through, or even to use his gun against the policemen, he shot himself instead."

Stunned, the police officers realized they had stumbled onto something. Fleischmann was handcuffed, Kallos's knapsack searched. In it were the earphones to Hannah's transmitter.

Fleischmann was whisked to police headquarters. He was beaten until he passed out, but he revealed nothing. A squadron of German soldiers was dispatched to search the area where Fleischmann and Kallos had first been spotted.

Hannah and Jacques waited in the woods. Something had gone wrong. That much was clear. But what? And what should they do? When almost three hours had passed, they felt they could wait no longer. They made their way to the road leading to the village just in time to see a group of soldiers heading toward them.

Retreating to the woods, they buried the transmitter and raced on. They realized, however, that they could not get away. The woods were being combed by soldiers who were advancing quickly, weapons drawn. They would certainly find them soon. Just as the soldiers burst upon them, Hannah and Jacques embraced, pretending to be lovers.

It almost worked. The commander wasn't sure what to make of them. He had them arrested and taken to headquarters "just in case." If they were really innocent, he said, they could resume their tryst the next day. Meanwhile soldiers continued to comb the forests and the fields beyond for the transmitter that went with the earphones from Kallos's knapsack. They destroyed the crops of neighboring farms and searched the ground. Their perseverance paid off. After two days, they found the transmitter.

Now the commander was sure that Hannah and Jacques were not innocent lovers, but had been in the woods because they were part of an underground group of some kind. He was determined to make them talk.

He placed Hannah and Jacques in separate cells and interrogated Hannah himself. Unable to get any answers from her, he tried to trap her. "It doesn't matter whether you tell us anything or not," he said. "We know enough already. One of the boys has confessed everything and he'll be executed tomorrow."

Hannah took the bait. "He had absolutely nothing to do with the matter," she said. "The radio is mine."

The officer demanded to know the code to the radio, what communications Hannah had received on it, and from whom. Hannah refused to tell him. She was beaten black and blue. One front tooth was knocked out. The soles of her feet and the palms of her hands were whipped until they bled. "They asked her one thing, only one thing," Yoel remembered Hannah telling him later. "What is your radio code? . . . they . . . wanted to use it to send out false information, to mislead bomber squadrons so that they could be greeted by fighters and anti-aircraft guns."

After three days, battered beyond recognition, Hannah was handcuffed, placed under heavy guard, and sent on the train to Budapest. She had remained silent and given the police no information. But as the train raced along, she must have felt she would not be able to hold out much longer. If Reuven had given her the cyanide, perhaps she would have taken it then. Some miles outside of Budapest, she tried to hurl herself from the window of the speeding train. One of the guards caught her and pulled her inside. "You are state property," he said. "We'll do away with you when we no longer need you, not before."

From the Budapest railway station, on the sixteenth of June, Hannah was taken to the Horthy Miklos Street Military Prison, where she was beaten again. Her hair was pulled out in fistfuls, her hands and feet whipped, her body and face punched and battered. She told her interrogators her name. But she did not reveal the code to the radio.

"June 17," Catherine Senesh wrote years later, "I got up at about eight and began dressing. The bell rang. I hurried to the window and saw a stranger who, on catching sight of me said, 'I'm looking for Mrs. Bela . . . Senesh . . . I'm a State Police Detective. Please open the door.' "

Catherine showed the man into the entrance hall.

"You're being summoned to the office of Military Headquarters as a witness," he said. "Please come along."

"Witness for whom?" Catherine asked. "In what matter?"

"I don't know," the man answered.

Catherine asked the detective to wait. She rushed upstairs to Margit Dayka, a very well-known actress who had been renting a part of Catherine's home for the past two years. Margit was not Jewish, but "in those tragic days," Catherine wrote, she "demonstrated infinite sympathy for those of us who were being hunted, and was unfailingly helpful and kind."

Margit had chosen to stay with Catherine even after the German occupation in March, and the rush of humiliating laws, horrifying rumors, confusion and fear that followed. Although the Jews of Budapest had not been rounded up and arrested en masse, they had been set apart from other Hungarians, and forced to wear the Yellow Star of David on their clothing. They were forbidden to leave their homes except at certain times of day. Jewish stores and offices had been ordered closed—as a protection against looting, according to the Minister of Justice. Automobiles, radios, books, art objects, even clothing belonging to Jews had been confiscated. Telephones had been removed from Jewish homes. The Food Ministry prohibited Jews from purchasing butter, eggs or rice. It restricted the amount of milk and meat they could obtain. Jewish bank deposits had been frozen, and Jews were not allowed to have in their possession more than 3,000 pengo (about $700) in ready cash. They were not allowed to travel. They were not allowed to own weapons of any kind. The publication of works by Jewish authors had been prohibited.

With every passing day, it seemed to Catherine, she heard

about someone who had been arrested for no known reason, someone who had disappeared, someone who had committed suicide. Her sister had made her way to Budapest before the ban on Jewish travel, and Catherine was greatly relieved to have her nearby. But they worried about their relatives in the provinces, whom they could no longer visit. Catherine heard that Jews in the countryside were being shunted into ghettoes and camps. Then she heard rumors that they were being transported to "unknown destinations." Wild speculations were everywhere, and some of Catherine's friends were trying to flee. At the beginning of May 1944, when the Jews of Budapest were told to prepare to move into special "Yellow Star" houses, Catherine too "packed a few essentials, ready for any eventuality, but was uncertain what to do."

Old friends urged Catherine to obtain false identity papers and escape with them to Rumania and then to Palestine. "I thought the plan unfeasible," Catherine wrote, "even absurd, yet out of desperation agreed and obtained the forged papers. But I had not as yet reached a definite decision."

On the thirteenth of June, a few days before the detective's call, the Gestapo had come to requisition the Senesh home. They "had only been prevented from doing so by her [Margit's] heated intervention," Catherine wrote. The women decided to go to the Housing Authority and place the house in Margit's name entirely. On the very day they planned to go, the detective came to the house and demanded that Catherine come with him.

"Hearing what had happened," Catherine wrote, "she [Margit] threw on a dressing gown, rushed downstairs, and asked the detective to be seated in the drawing room. She tried to find out why I was being taken for questioning but could obtain no information either."

Catherine was taken by tram to Military Headquarters in Horthy Miklos Boulevard, a trip of about half an hour. As she recalled later, she was curious as well as frightened, "since I could not imagine why they wanted me." At least, Catherine said to herself, her children were far away and safe. That was "the only thing of great importance . . . and that was assured. Whatever happened to me did not matter."

The detective was courteous, even friendly, and chatted with Catherine about Margit's career, the plays and movies in which she had starred, her plans for the future. "He was really quite . . . considerate," Catherine wrote, "and immediately agreed when I asked permission to telephone Margit." It seemed more important than ever that the house be put in the actress's name, and Catherine wanted to make sure Margit would see to it without delay.

When they left the tram, Catherine stopped at a small shop to make the call, but as she began to dial, the owner shouted at her to stop. "What's the matter with you!" he yelled. "Don't you know anyone wearing a Yellow Star is forbidden to use a public phone?"

Catherine hadn't known, and neither had the detective. He said she could use the phone in his office.

At Military Headquarters, Catherine was left in a small room on the second floor with two police officers while the detective went to tell his superiors that she had arrived. The police, Catherine recalled, were having a mid-morning snack of smoked bacon and green peppers. When the detective returned he asked them to leave, showed Catherine to a telephone, and when she had finished her call, asked her whether she had any children.

"When I replied in the affirmative, he asked where they were. There happened to be a large map on the wall and I smilingly pointed to Palestine."

Just then the door opened. "A very tall civilian of military bearing entered the room," Catherine wrote. He introduced himself simply as "Rozsa." Then he pointed to a chair and motioned for Catherine to sit down while he settled himself behind a typewriter. The interrogation began. Rozsa asked Catherine some routine questions about the Senesh family and about George. Then he turned his attention to Hannah. "Much to my surprise," Catherine wrote, "he questioned me endlessly about her, stopped the pretense of typing, and asked what specific reasons she had had for leaving home. 'I can understand a boy leaving home,' he said, 'to see the world, to complete his studies, to prepare for his career. But a girl . . . why should a young girl want to leave her home, her mother, her friends?' "

Catherine answered the questions candidly, without feeling at all intimidated. "For all the reasons you mentioned," she replied. "Jewish youth has no future in Hungary . . . And much as it hurt me to part with her, particularly after having had to part with my son, I'm happy she's not here now to see and experience the terrible suffering of the Jews."

At this, "a scornful smile spread over his unpleasant face," Catherine wrote, and then the interrogation continued: What had Hannah been doing for the past few years? Where was she at present? What was she doing now? "Above all," Catherine recalled, he wanted to know "how, from where, and how often I received news from her. The thought struck me that perhaps one of her letters had been intercepted and contained something that displeased the censor."

The interrogation picked up speed. Catherine recalled the barrage of questions: "What had Hannah done before leaving Budapest? Who were her friends? Her teachers? What had she been interested in? With what had she primarily concerned herself? What profession had she thought of following? What were her ambitions?"

Still Catherine was not flustered. "Perhaps you'll construe this merely as a mother's normal pride in her child," she said after one barrage of questions, "but I can tell you my daughter is an unusually gifted girl and in every respect a very remarkable young woman. You need not take my word. You can question her teachers who will, I am sure, verify my statements."

Finally Rozsa seemed satisfied. He told the detective to type a summary of what Catherine had said. She would have to sign it and swear under oath that her testimony had been the truth. Catherine said she would, and Rozsa left the room while the detective finished typing. When Rozsa came back, he read the statement carefully, made Catherine swear to its truth and watched her sign it.

"Now then," he said, leaning toward her. "Where do you *really* think your daughter is now—this minute?"

Catherine remembered replying that "to the best of my knowledge she was on an agricultural settlement in the vicinity of Haifa."

"Well, if you really don't know," Rozsa said, "I'll tell you. She's here, in the adjoining room. I'll bring her right in so you can talk to her and persuade her to tell us everything she knows. Because if she doesn't—this will be your last meeting."

"I felt as if the floor were giving way under me," Catherine wrote, "and clutched the edge of the table frantically with both hands. My eyes closed, and in a matter of seconds I felt everything —hope, faith, trust, the very meaning of life, everything I had ever believed in—collapse like a child's house of cards. I was completely shattered, physically and spiritually."

The door opened. Catherine turned toward it. Four men led Hannah in.

"Had I not known she was coming," Catherine wrote, "perhaps in that first moment I would not have recognized the Hannah of five years ago. Her once soft, wavy hair hung in a filthy tangle, her ravaged face reflected untold suffering, her large, expressive eyes were blackened, and there were ugly welts on her cheeks and neck. That was my first glimpse of her."

Hannah ran to Catherine. "She . . . threw her arms around my neck," Catherine wrote, "sobbing, 'Mother, forgive me!'

"I felt the pounding of her heart and her scalding tears. At the same time I noted the expectant, avid expressions on the faces of the staring men as they watched us—as if they had been watching a scene in a play. Again the floor seemed to sway, and it took all my strength to maintain my self-control and remain silent."

"Speak to her!" Rozsa snapped. "Convince her she had better tell us everything, otherwise you'll never see each other again."

"I had not the faintest idea what was happening," Catherine

wrote. "Not even in my wildest imaginings would it have occurred to me that Hannah . . . was a volunteer in the British Army. Nor did I know a woman could become a member of the British Armed forces. What puzzled me was how she had suddenly been catapulted from the far distance into the hell that was then Hungary. . . . no one told me anything, or explained anything, and I could not possibly have guessed the truth. But of one thing I was absolutely certain: if there was something Hannah did not want to reveal, she had good reason, and under no circumstances would I influence her otherwise."

"Well," Rozsa snarled, "why don't you talk?"

Catherine held Hannah. "There is no need to repeat yourself," she said. "We both heard you." Her voice sounded strange to her.

The soldiers ordered the women to be seated in facing chairs. They and Rozsa left the room.

"We couldn't find words," Catherine wrote. "Then suddenly it occurred to me that Hannah, upon hearing about the horrible things happening to the Jews in Hungary, might have volunteered for a daring, even reckless mission, in an effort to rescue me. I was only too familiar with her extraordinary courage, will-power and perseverance when faced with seemingly insurmountable obstacles. And regardless of the considerable distance between us, I was always aware of her love and constant concern. 'Hannah,' [I said,] 'tell me, am I the cause of what's happening here? Did anxiety about me bring you back?' She quickly reassured me. 'No, Mother! No!' she said. 'You're not to blame for anything.' 'But how did you get here?' I asked. 'I received a telegram not long ago to say that George had arrived in Palestine. Isn't he there now either?' "

Hannah assured her that he was. "I sent the telegram myself," she said. "You needn't worry about George, believe me. He's fine."

"I noticed one of her upper teeth was missing, obviously a result of the same beating that had produced the welts and bruises on her face and neck. . . . Seeing her in such battered condition was heartbreaking. I stroked her hands, the nails broken, the skin like sandpaper. The purple-black bruises on her face were like knife wounds in my own flesh, and I leaned over to kiss her."

At this Rozsa and the soldiers rushed back in. They had evidently been spying.

"He [Rozsa] pushed us apart," Catherine wrote, and said, " 'Whispering is not allowed here! Anyway, that's enough for today.' "

The soldiers stepped forward. "They took Hannah away," Catherine wrote, "and Rozsa turned back to me. 'I could detain you as well,' [he said,] 'but I'm taking your age into consideration. Go on home! If we have further need of you we'll telephone. . . . But I warn you, you're not to tell anyone anything that has happened here today. Not a word! Not even that you've set foot inside this building. Understand?' "

Rozsa left the office. The detective saw that Catherine was barely able to move. "Rest a moment," he said. "We don't have to leave immediately."

"His kindness gave me courage to ask what was going on," Catherine wrote. "But he protested he didn't know."

Nevertheless he tried to comfort her. "Don't take the threats too seriously," he said. "Things don't happen quite that fast around here. Everything will be straightened out—you'll see."

"I stumbled home," Catherine wrote. "It must have been about one in the afternoon. A small group of neighbors . . . were waiting . . . with Margit. They ran toward me, clamoring to know what had happened. 'It was all a misunderstanding,' I told them."

Later Margit told Catherine's sister she had changed utterly in the few hours she'd been away. "She had difficulty believing," Catherine wrote, "I was the same woman who had left with the detective that morning."

CHAPTER 12

AUGUST

*"I was crying for my child,
for her youth,
for her cruel predicament
and probably hopeless fate"*

MARGIT and Catherine had just gone inside when a limousine arrived to take Margit to her film studio. She did not want to leave Catherine alone, but Catherine begged her to go. "[I] promised if anything happened I would somehow get word to her," Catherine wrote. "All I wanted was to be left alone."

Margit had no sooner left, however, than the doorbell rang. It was Catherine's friend, the man who had urged her to obtain false identity papers so she could escape from Hungary with him and his family. He had come to see how she was getting along with her preparations, explaining that he thought they should try to leave within the next day or two. "I told him firmly," Catherine recalled, "that after giving the matter most careful consideration I had decided not to leave Budapest." He urged her to reconsider, detailing the "bright prospects of life in Palestine," especially for Catherine, since her children were there! "If there is anyone to whom it's worth the risk and the gamble," he said, "you're certainly the one."

As he spoke, Catherine realized she could tell him what had happened. He was a serious, level-headed man, and she knew he could be "trusted absolutely" with her secret. And if he and his wife ever reached Palestine, they could tell George the whole story. "I felt as if Providence had sent him," she wrote. "I so desperately needed someone to confide in . . ."

The man listened with "rigid attention" to Catherine's story. "This is really a catastrophe," he said at last, "and of course I understand now why you don't want to leave. It's difficult to find an explanation for what has happened." He assured Catherine that he would not tell anyone, but he urged her to confide "in those who might possibly be able to help you. First of all," he said, "I think you ought to tell Margit, who probably has connections in military circles."

Catherine, though, did not have the chance to tell anyone else. As she was saying goodbye to her friend, the doorbell rang again. From the window, Catherine could see a car at the curb, surrounded by SS men. Then one of them called: "We are looking for Mrs. Senesh. Please let us in."

Quickly, Catherine hid the forged identification papers she had taken out to show her friend. Then she unlocked the door. Gestapo Captain Seifert entered with four SS men. After questioning Catherine's friend briefly, Seifert allowed him to leave. Then he told Catherine that she would have to "come along immediately for interrogation."

Catherine stalled for time, hoping her housekeeper would return before she was taken away. The housekeeper would be able to tell Margit of Catherine's arrest, and Margit would tell Catherine's sister. "I can't possibly leave now," she said to Seifert, hoping to seem naïve. "I'm entirely responsible for the house and personal belongings of Margit Dayka, the actress, and she's not at home."

Seifert was not impressed. "Just get ready," he said.

"I went to my room slowly," Catherine wrote, "Seifert on my heels." Clearly, the Gestapo Captain did not know that she had already been questioned by the Hungarian police. Catherine wondered if she should tell him. Would that make things better for Hannah, or worse? "Remembering Rozsa's threatening tone," Catherine wrote, "I decided to say nothing."

Seifert followed Catherine from room to room, hurrying her along. Suddenly, he held out a photograph. "Do you recognize this girl?" he asked. It was a picture of Hannah as Catherine had seen her that morning, her face bruised and swollen almost beyond recognition. She pretended not to know her.

Seifert put the photograph away and continued to hurry Catherine. She had run out of excuses and was about to lock up the house when the housekeeper returned. "I was able to exchange a few words with her," Catherine wrote. "I gave her Margit's number, and asked her to telephone her immediately after I left. She, on the other hand, knowing I had not yet eaten anything that day, rushed to the kitchen, prepared a few sandwiches, and slipped them into my large handbag."

Seifert briskly led Catherine to the waiting car, which took her directly to the German Police Prison. There she was led upstairs and delivered into the presence of a "gaunt, fearsome looking young SS man with a Death's Head badge on his cap." ("Death's Head Units"—Totenkopfverbande—were the guard units at concentration and death camps. Members were selected for their viciousness and lack of compassion, qualities Hitler considered virtues.) As the SS man grimly examined all her belongings and confiscated her wallet, fountain pen, watch and wedding ring, Catherine observed that his "face resembled his badge." After looking through her wallet, he asked her whether she had any more money.

"I wore a little bag around my neck," she later wrote, "in which I carried the maximum amount of money Jews were allowed. After an instant's hesitation, I handed it to him. The reward for the momentary delay was a powerful slap across my face."

The slap sent Catherine spinning completely around. "But

strangely enough," she noted, "[I] didn't feel the blow at all. After that morning's encounter with Hannah I felt nothing: as if a stranger had taken my place, or a mechanized puppet."

A record was made of Catherine's belongings, and she was told that everything would be returned to her when and if she was released. Then she was led to her cell. "The lock of a heavy steel door creaked open, and I stepped into a surprisingly spacious, bright room," she recalled. It had six white iron beds, and apart from the bars on the window, it looked more like a hospital ward than the prison cell she had imagined. "A number of inquisitive-looking women turned expectantly toward me, but I soon learned they always did this—and so would I—upon the arrival of a new 'roomer.'"

Catherine realized she knew one of the women, the Baroness Böske Hatvany, who seemed to be the accepted leader. Böske introduced Catherine to the others. There was Mrs. Eugene Vida, wife of the only Jewish member of Parliament. Her ex-butler had denounced her for making an anti-Nazi remark. The Countess Zichy, also Jewish, had been arrested while attempting to hide valuable paintings from the Germans. The widow of Lehel Hédervráy had been arrested for collaborating with the Allies. "They all wondered how I came to be among them," Catherine wrote. "After all, I was not a member of the moneyed aristocracy, nor politically involved. . . . Of course, I didn't dare reveal the reason for my imprisonment."

Some of the women were playing bridge, using cards Böske had fashioned from scraps of paper. Catherine watched them silently. Later, an argument broke out over the Countess Zichy's refusal to take her turn cleaning the room and adjoining toilet. Catherine barely followed it. "Due to my state of mind," she wrote, "I was not yet able to make contact with prison life; my thoughts were certainly elsewhere. I crouched in a corner, and remained silent."

The next day, worry over Hannah "weighed so heavily" on Catherine that she told her story to Böske, who listened "in shocked silence." Still, Catherine felt remote from her surroundings, unable to focus on or care about what was going on around her. She observed things "through a haze of preoccupation," she wrote, "my thoughts wholly centered upon Hannah, wondering whether she was still alive. Certainly she would never divulge what they wanted to know, and they would show no mercy."

That night, Catherine was overwhelmed by despair. Told she could expect to be interrogated the next day, she felt trapped, impotent, hopeless. Even if her daughter was still alive, there was no way Catherine could help her. What was the point of going through the "further torment" that the next day's interrogation would surely be? Searching through her cellmates' belongings, she found Countess Zichy's razor blade, which was used as a knife, pencil sharpener and scissors. Taking it to bed with her, she waited until everyone seemed to be asleep. Then, finding the main artery in her wrist, she slashed her wrist. "It [the blood] did not gush forth as I expected," she wrote, so she slashed again. But again, there was only a trickle of blood. Then Böske saw her. "Fearfully she rushed over and grabbed my wrist," Catherine wrote. "Tightly binding it with two small handkerchiefs," Böske berated Catherine for her foolishness, and advised her to wear long sleeves when she went for her interrogation so that the Germans would not see what she had done.

On her third day in prison, Catherine was taken to Gestapo headquarters at Schwab Hill. She waited in the crowded corridor there until nightfall, but she was not questioned, nor was she told anything about Hannah or her own release. That evening, however, when she was returned to the prison, she was advised that she would be allowed to send one postcard to anyone she chose. "This would be my one and only opportunity," she wrote, "to notify someone of my whereabouts, and to ask for food parcels, clothing and toilet articles." Not wishing to jeopardize her sister's or Margit's safety, Catherine addressed her postcard to a hairdresser in her neighborhood, and asked her to "please give it to the lady who lives in my house."

Each day the number of prisoners in Catherine's cell increased. Soon the once spacious room was filled with twenty women. Catherine spoke freely about Hannah now, asking every new roomer whether they had seen or heard of her daughter. But no one knew anything. Then, at the end of her first week in prison, as Catherine was being whisked down the corridor for her second visit to Schwab Hill, a young prisoner scrubbing the floor whispered to her: "Auntie* Kate, Hannah is here too. I talked to her last night."

"I could barely control myself," Catherine wrote. But "I was only too well aware that talking was strictly forbidden," so Catherine kept moving, in silence.

This time Catherine was taken straight into the interrogation room where she was questioned by Gestapo Captain Seifert. There was no need for Catherine to admit that her daughter had indeed been the girl in the photograph. Captain Seifert did not question her further about it or treat her disrespectfully. Instead his manner was so courteous that Catherine found the courage to ask him what exactly was going on, what the charges were against Hannah, and what was going to be done to her.

"He weighed my questions silently," Catherine wrote, "and finally, instead of answering directly, said, 'According to my interpretation of Hungarian law, your daughter's life is in no danger. German laws are more stringent.' "

Catherine felt as though she could "breathe more easily." That very night, a young prisoner named Hilda, who had been assigned to office work and who was often entrusted with errands of "great responsibility," unlocked the door to Catherine's cell and called her into the corridor.

"She whispered that [when I returned to my cell,] I was to stand by the window of the cell and look across. . . . I did as she bid. . . . At the window directly across the yard, and exactly opposite mine, I saw Hannah. She smiled and waved."

After a minute, Hannah disappeared, but the next morning Catherine stationed herself at the window again and shortly after

*It was cutomary in Hungary for young people to call older people "uncle" and "aunt," even when they were not actually relatives.

dawn, Hannah appeared. She traced the letters for "good morning" in the air and Catherine answered in the same way. Thus they had their first talk in prison.

Catherine's cellmates came to the window to watch the "conversation." Hannah noted the Yellow Stars on their clothing and asked what they meant. After Catherine explained, one of the other prisoners wrote her own message in the air to Hannah: "You're lucky not to be branded." Immediately, Hannah drew an enormous Star of David on her dust-coated window. "As soon as she had drawn the Star," Catherine wrote, "she disappeared from the window, and although I watched for her all day she did not appear again."

The next evening, Hilda returned to Catherine's cell. In a whisper, she told Catherine to hurry to the bathroom, for she had just taken Hannah there. They would be able to have a few minutes together. With tears in her eyes, Catherine rushed off.

"At last I could hold her close, kiss her," Catherine wrote. In response to her mother's urgent questions, Hannah explained that she had been a radio officer in the British Army, and had volunteered for a mission that "unfortunately" she had been unable to complete. "I'm reconciled to my fate," she said. "But the thought that I've needlessly involved you in all this is unbearable."

Catherine held her and comforted her. There was, she said, one important consolation for the fact that she too had been arrested. "I could be close to her, could see her now and again, even talk to her. Had I been allowed to remain free I would probably not have been able to obtain visiting privileges, and there could even have been the horrible possibility of deportation and separation forever."

Hannah smiled sadly. For a minute, she seemed to Catherine to look almost like her old self. The bruises from the beatings had healed. Her hair was clean. Her expression was calm. But the gap in her mouth disturbed Catherine, and she couldn't help but ask about it. "Dearest Mother," Hannah said, laughing "if all I lose during this venture is a single tooth, we can both be really grateful." She had just begun to tell Catherine how the suicide of one of the boys in her group had "triggered the subsequent catastrophe" when Hilda came in and told them they would have to part.

For the next several weeks, Catherine rarely saw Hannah at all, not even in the window. She soon learned that her daughter was being taken to "the Hill" early every morning and kept there for interrogation until nightfall. Some of Catherine's cellmates met Hannah in the police van when they were being taken to the Hill or in the waiting room at the interrogation center itself. They reported that she was in good spirits, eager to talk to them about Palestine and to help them maintain their faith in the future. She shared parts of her story with them, and they passed it on. From them, Catherine learned the outlines of Hannah's mission—the parachute drop into Yugoslavia, the months with the partisans.

Sometimes Hannah appeared in her window first thing in the morning. Instead of writing letters in the air, she held up huge letters that she had fashioned out of scrap paper. Catherine quickly did the same, and soon they were both expert at this method of communication. Both of them were careful to stand a few feet back from the window so that their messages could only be observed by someone looking directly into the cell, not by the guards in the yard below. Sometimes, though, in the middle of a message, Hannah would suddenly duck down and not be seen again. Catherine later found out that Hannah could reach her window only by putting a table on her bed, and a chair on top of the table. The chair was brought in each morning for Hannah to use as a washstand, then it was taken out again. When Hannah heard the guard coming to retrieve it, she had to jump down quickly from the window and place the chair back beside the door. After that, it was impossible for her to communicate with her mother.

On days when Hannah was not being interrogated Catherine was able to see her walking in the yard after lunch. "Or, to put it more accurately," Catherine wrote, "I could watch one corner of the yard, for as the line turned I could catch a momentary glimpse of her in that corner." The other prisoners in Hannah's exercise group walked in pairs, but as a prisoner in solitary confinement, Hannah had to walk alone at the end of the line. Though she couldn't see Catherine, she knew Catherine could see her, and as she reached the corner, she would look up in the direction of Catherine's cell.

On one occasion, Catherine's group happened to be in the yard for exercise at the same time as Hannah's. "By then," Catherine wrote, "the majority of the inmates knew us or had heard about us. Consequently everyone who was aware of our relationship watched excitedly to see if we could manage a meeting, an exchange of words." But it seemed hopeless. Catherine was at the head of her double column, Hannah was alone at the tail end of hers. "The matron stood in the center of the vast yard, watchful; the armed military guards were stationed at various points."

Repeatedly, Catherine saw Hannah drop out of line, "evidently troubled by her shoelace." Each time she stopped she took a step backward, until at last she was right beside Catherine. "My partner stepped back," Catherine wrote, "and Hannah slipped into her place. It was done so smoothly, so effortlessly, one would have thought it had been carefully rehearsed." Catherine and Hannah chatted softly as the walk continued, although whenever the matron looked in their direction, Catherine froze and swallowed her words.

Meanwhile, on June 29, Hannah's fourteenth day of imprisonment, Yoel Palgi had been brought to the German Police Prison. He had been in Budapest for two weeks before he was arrested—weeks spent with members of the Jewish underground, and in the hope that Hannah might yet keep their rendezvous. Following his arrest, he had been taken to the Hungarian Army Prison and beaten savagely. As he wrote later, he had no idea then that Hannah had already been arrested and he had consoled himself by thinking that "it's a good thing she [Hannah] doesn't have to suffer all this. . . . When she comes, she'll succeed where I failed . . . and the world won't be able to say there is no way of helping, no way of saving Jews."

It was one of Palgi's guards at the Hungarian Army Prison who inadvertently told him about Hannah. Seeing Palgi in his cell, blood-soaked and in tears "he took pity on me and came in to console me," Palgi wrote. The guard told him that "it would soon be over," that he wouldn't be tortured "indefinitely." When Palgi said he expected to be hung, the guard reassured him. "We don't hang people so easily, so don't worry," he said. "There was a girl here from Palestine a few days ago, and she was only sentenced to five years."

"The guard had meant to console me," Yoel wrote, "but I was shocked. I guessed that the five-year sentence was something he had just invented, but not the girl from Palestine; I knew it must be Hannah."

A few days later, Yoel was transferred to the German Police Prison and placed in solitary confinement. There, depressed and dispirited, he could hardly believe his ears when he suddenly heard a voice calling down the corridor: "Hannah Senesh!" and Hannah's voice replying, "Yes."

"I frantically pounded on my cell door with my fist," Yoel recalled, "kicked at it, stormed and raged. The door opened and the warden asked gruffly what I wanted." Yoel pushed him aside and rushed into the corridor. No one was there. He half-believed that he had imagined the call and Hannah's answer. But the next day, when he was taken to Schwab Hill for questioning, he asked the other prisoners whether they had seen Hannah or heard anything about a "Palestinian girl." One of them had not only heard of her, but had been with her the day before. She was "remarkable," he said to Yoel, "and tells everyone about Eretz Israel. She really gave us hope."

By this time—July 1944—437,402 Hungarian Jews had been sent to their deaths in Poland. The roundups, still restricted to the Jews in the countryside, were carried out by Hungarian police with great brutality. Children were whipped to make them climb more quickly into the waiting trains. Infants and disabled people were taken up bodily and hurled on board. People were stuffed into freight cars on top of one another because there was not enough room for them to stand. When the cars were packed full, they were sealed and the windows nailed shut. Thousands of people died before they even reached the gas chambers of Auschwitz, the largest death camp of all. Hannah's cousin, Evi Sas, was one of the 3,000,000 Jews murdered there.

Word of the roundups soon reached the outside world. Allied governments had known since 1942 that Jews who were taken from their homes were not "resettled" anywhere, as the Germans claimed, but killed. But though the Jews of Hungary were being rounded up and deported on orders from Germany, the operation was being carried out by Hungarian police forces. So it was to the Regent of Hungary, Miklos Horthy, that neutral countries, as well as the Vatican and the International Red Cross, sent telegrams and messages of protest. Pope Pius XII sent a letter to Horthy on June 25. President Roosevelt sent a note via the Swiss Embassy on June 26. The King of Sweden sent a message on June 30. American Secretary of State Cordell Hull threatened "reprisals" against those responsible, and Swedish and Swiss diplomats made heroic efforts to persuade Horthy to allow Jews to leave the country now that the Germans had taken over.

On July 4, Horthy appealed to Veesenmayer, his German overseer, to stop the deportations. Then, on July 6, Horthy took responsibility into his own hands and called a halt to them. He had just learned about a secret message sent by the Jewish underground to the American and British missions in Switzerland. The message, discovered by Hungarian spies, contained detailed information about the fate of the deported Jews—where and when and exactly how they were being killed. It named the Hungarian agencies that were helping to deport them and urged that they be bombed. Exact addresses of these agencies—house numbers and descriptions of roads—were included. Also included was a list of seventy Hungarians and Germans who were "most responsible" for the operation, along with their addresses. Horthy didn't know that the British and American embassies had received all this information weeks earlier and had not acted on it. Frightened at what he assumed the response would be, he issued the order to stop all deportations.

The situation between Germany and Hungary now grew more tense than it had ever been before. Veesenmayer threatened a total military occupation of Hungary if the deportations were not resumed. Horthy, noting that the Germans were in retreat on almost every front in Europe, and that the Russian Army was already in nearby Galicia, ignored the threat.

In prison, Catherine prepared for her daughter's twenty-third birthday. She had saved a small jar of marmalade from one of her food parcels from Margit, and she wrapped it now as a gift. The other women in her cell took things out from their own "precious stores": a handkerchief, a sliver of soap, a sponge. In prison, Catherine wrote, each of these things was a "cherished, rare possession." One of the matrons agreed to deliver the gifts, and later returned with a piece of paper upon which Hannah had written her thanks, adding that she had "summed up and weighed the events of her life" and that "looking back over her twenty-three years decided that they had been very colorful and eventful, her childhood happy and beautiful. Her accounting with life at such a tender age," wrote Catherine, "was like a dagger in my heart."

On July 23, almost a week after Hannah's birthday, the Russian Army, advancing across Poland, discovered Maidenek, the death camp near the city of Lublin in which 1,500,000 people had by that time been killed. At first the world did not believe what the Russians found there. Soviet writer Konstantin Simonov wrote a full description of Maidenek for the Russian newspaper *Pravda.* Two British newspapers, the *London Illustrated News* and the *Sphere,* picked up the story and published special issues about Maidenek, including photographs of human bones, the gas chambers and the ovens. But other newspapers and communications media, in Britain and elsewhere, did not disseminate the story, finding it "incredible." Alexander Werth, the British correspondent for the *Sunday Times,* sent his own detailed report to the British Broadcasting Company. The BBC refused to use it, saying that it sounded like a "Russian propaganda stunt." American newspapers and wire services would not accept the story either. The dimensions alone—the number of people reported killed, and the way in which they had been executed—made it seem, they said, impossible. The *New York Herald Tribune* summarized Werth's report, then commented: "Maybe we should wait for further corroboration of the horror story that comes from Lublin. Even on top of all we have been taught of the maniacal Nazi ruthlessness, this example sounds inconceivable."

On July 24, the day after the discovery of Maidenek, a record was set at the Auschwitz death camp: 46,000 people were gassed to death, the largest number ever murdered on a single day.

In the German Police Prison in Budapest toward the end of July, children appeared at Hannah's side during exercise periods. Catherine watched her window, happy to see them, knowing that Hannah must be pleased too. They played around her as she walked, grabbed her arms, held her hands. Two in particular struck Catherine. They were, she learned, Polish. The boy and girl, one eight and the other six, had been wandering with their mother from camp to camp, prison to prison, for years. "They immediately sensed a friend in Hannah and would not leave her side," Catherine wrote. Sometimes they even played tag as the guards "benevolently" looked the other way.

To please these children, Hannah began making dolls, "concocting them ingeniously from bits and pieces of string, papers, rags, crayons." For a few days, she was allowed to stay in the children's cell, though Catherine never found out how this had been arranged, or by whom. But she did hear that Hannah was teaching the children to read and write, played with them constantly, told them stories, "entertained them with anecdotes and songs about Palestine." Then, as suddenly as she had become the children's cellmate, she was removed and put back into solitary confinement. She continued, however, to make the dolls, and her "window correspondence" with Catherine resumed once again.

Now Hannah wondered whether Catherine might like to learn Hebrew, pointing out that she would never have a better opportunity, considering all the time she had on her hands. "Though I was not exactly in the mood to study anything," Catherine wrote, "I knew if I agreed she would be pleased. From then on excellently organized and prepared lessons arrived daily."

One morning, when Hannah was perched on the chair sending messages to her mother, the door to her cell burst open and a guard named Marietta stormed in. She was, Catherine remembered, "the most dreaded and implacable" of all the matrons in charge of women prisoners—so cruel that many prisoners gave up the longed-for ten-minute walk in the yard if Marietta was on yard duty. "She used to stand in the center of the yard, bullwhip in hand like an animal trainer in the circus, directing the prisoners." Marietta began shouting at Hannah "at the top of her strong voice," demanding she reveal the name of her contact. Hannah shouted back—in "equally energetic tones"—that her "contact" was her mother!

Marietta left without another word, but from then on, whenever she came on duty, the first thing she did was bring a chair to Hannah's room. "This same Marietta," Catherine wrote, also assembled "a package with an exceptionally fine assortment of delicacies pilfered from other prisoners' parcels and sent it to her [Hannah]." She also brought Hannah the materials she needed to make her dolls. "Gradually more and more of her dolls turned up," Catherine recalled, "and the more she made the more ingenious, varied and colorful they became." Hannah sent them to the prisoners and also to the matrons—intricate and lovely Biedermeier dolls, rococo dolls, ballet dancer dolls, Carmens, Madame Butterfly dolls, Toscas and others. But most popular were her Palestine dolls, boy and girl pioneers, carrying picks and shovels on their shoulders.

By August, Hannah's silent conversations were no longer directed only at Catherine. Her window had become a general information and support center, an "education center," according to Yoel Palgi, and "from morning till evening prisoners looked toward it for news." Other prisoners whom Hannah saw on her trips to the Hill, especially those newly arrived from the "outside world," passed information to her. Hannah listened carefully for news from the guards and in turn passed on everything she learned to others. Her messages "were watched for avidly by every prisoner whose window faced the yard," wrote Catherine, especially the young Zionists whose window was directly opposite Hannah's. They had been arrested for underground activities and were awaiting sentence. Hannah encouraged them tremendously, cheered them up and "gave them new heart." "I was distressed by her courage and recklessness," wrote Catherine, "afraid that her already precarious situation would be aggravated if her foolhardy actions came to the attention of the Commandant. But my warnings had no effect upon her."

Yoel too found Hannah's behavior with the Gestapo and SS "quite remarkable." She "always stood up to them," he wrote, even going so far as to warn "them plainly of the bitter fate they would suffer after their defeat." These "wild animals," he wrote, "in whom every spark of humanity had been extinguished, felt awed in the presence of this refined, fearless young girl. They knew she was Jewish, but they also knew she was a British paratrooper who had come to fight them. . . . they were taken aback by her courage."

One August evening, four new prisoners were brought to Catherine's already overcrowded cell. Two of them, hardly more than children, had been arrested at the Hungarian frontier as they attempted to flee the country. They had already been taken to Schwab Hill for questioning and were eager to talk about what had happened to them. One of them asked whether any of the women knew "a charming and knowledgeable young woman prisoner who greets new prisoners and gives them advice, encourages them, tells them how to answer questions, and seems to have a great deal of information about everything."

Catherine smiled. "That's Hannah," one of her cellmates said. "Kate's daughter. She's not afraid of anything or anyone, and knows everything."

Catherine's wedding anniversary fell during the first week of August. That year was her twenty-fifth, her silver anniversary. Although she herself had long since stopped celebrating anniversaries, during "that sad August in prison," Hannah remembered the occasion. She covered an empty talcum powder can with silver foil. Then she pulled twenty-five blades of straw from her mattress and to them attached twenty-five white buds made of tissue paper. These "flowers" she fitted into the holes in the top of the powder can, "which then looked like a delightful little bouquet of white roses." She glued a lace doily, also made of tissue paper, to the bottom of the can. Accompanying the flowers was "an exquisite little paper doll bride with a long veil, carrying a minute bouquet of tissue paper roses." Hannah sent a poem, too, which Catherine later remembered this way:

> Memories, like paper flowers
> Remain forever fresh.
> One often longingly studies them,
> The while forgetting
> They are not alive.

By mid-August, the prison was alive with news of an impending German withdrawal. The war was indeed going badly for Germany on every front. The Allies had advanced steadily through France, and were now within striking distance of Paris. The Soviets had broken through Rumania's defenses and it seemed it would not be long before they would be at Hungary's border. Although Eichmann had set August 27 as the date on which he would round up the Jews of Budapest, on August 20 he left the city for a secluded mountain retreat. And although Hungarian Nazis, particularly the Hungarian Nazi Arrow Cross Party, plotted behind the scenes to overthrow Horthy's government, for the time being Horthy could not be toppled. Allied victory was in the air, and attempts by the Hungarian government to please the Allies and dissociate Hungary from the Germans were evident. Horthy appointed Geza Lakatos, a strong anti-German, to be his new Prime Minister. Lakatos immediately disarmed the Hungarian gendarmerie, the forces that had rounded up the provincial Jews with such viciousness. Horthy himself assured the Jewish Council that the Jews of Budapest would not be deported, and Lakatos announced that henceforth Hungary would make its own decisions about the "Jewish question." A group of Hungarian officials was dispatched to Moscow to discuss an armistice. A series of legal measures was passed that, though small in itself, was intended to show the goodwill of the Hungarian government toward the Jews. Some Jewish stores were allowed to reopen. Curfews for Jews were relaxed.

Inside the German Police Prison, discipline was lightened. The rapidly advancing Russians were on everyone's mind, and the end of the war seemed at hand. Most of the prisoners now hoped—and expected—that they would soon be transferred to Kistarcsa, the Hungarian internment camp on the outskirts of Budapest, and from there, processed out and sent home. Everyone believed that the worst was already behind them. But Catherine sensed that her daughter was still in danger.

"One exceptionally quiet and beautiful night," Catherine wrote, "I found it impossible to sleep, and had the distinct feeling Hannah was not sleeping either. I crept to the window, fearful I would wake someone in the still night. The moon was shining so brightly it was almost like daylight, and I clearly saw Hannah silhouetted against the half-opened window wearing her light blue dressing gown, her hair softly framing her lovely face. She was entirely lost in thought, and the moon appeared to form a soft halo around her head. It seemed to me her soul was mirrored in her face at that instant. Overwhelmed by infinite sadness, I returned to my bed, fell upon it, and buried my head in my arms to stifle my sobs. I was crying for my child, for her youth, for her cruel predicament and probably hopeless fate."

Hannah had been told she would be allowed to spend time with her mother once the Germans were finished interrogating her. Now they were, but when she asked the Commandant to move her to her mother's cell or near it, he brushed off her request, saying he "had not been authorized" to change anything. As the days went by, Hannah asked again and again, insisting "with increasing vehemence," Catherine recalled, and finally, at the beginning of September, Hannah's cell was changed. She was not permitted to room with her mother, but she was placed in a cell on the same floor. She and Catherine were allowed to take their daily walk in the same group and sometimes to walk together. Thus they were able to have "brief, whispered conversations."

Perhaps the most wonderful thing about the new cell arrangement had to do with the communal water tap. It was in the corridor directly opposite Catherine's cell and she could see it from the window in the door. Three times a day, one prisoner from each cell was allowed to come to the tap to fetch water. Everyone competed for this job, since it was one of the only chances the prisoners had of leaving their "hated confinement." But the women in Hannah's cell, knowing it would give Catherine a chance to see her, gave Hannah exclusive rights to the job.

"I was able to look at her frequently," Catherine wrote, "and she would signal to me. There were even times when a matron would call me into the corridor under some pretext when Hannah was at the tap, thus giving me an opportunity to embrace her, to hold her in my arms."

Food, always a favorite topic in prison, became the primary topic among the cheerful, confident prisoners. Recipes for exotic gourmet dishes were discussed endlessly. One of the prisoners, the wife of a bank president, invited everyone to a "sumptuous supper" in the near future, so positive was she that they would all be free soon. But another prisoner, a Polish woman from the city of Krakow, went about "puncturing our lovely daydreams," Catherine wrote. "What folly," the woman said. "Most of us will probably end up in Auschwitz."

"Auschwitz?" Catherine wondered. "What was that? It was the first time I had ever heard about the Nazi extermination camps."

On August 27, the date Eichmann had originally set for the deportation of Budapest's Jews, German soldiers appeared and silently took up stations in and around the city. Prime Minister Lakatos, in alarm, ordered the arrest of Ferenc Szálasi, the Arrow Cross leader he knew was plotting against the government. But Szálasi was under the protection of the Germans and could not be touched. Horthy sent a message to Eichmann, noting the arrival of German soldiers and reminding him that Hungary would not allow deportations to be resumed. On September 7, he officially announced that the Hungarian government was in the process of seeking an armistice. On that same day, Horthy dispatched soldiers to prisons and internment camps—including the German Police Prison. Their orders were to protect Hungarian subjects and not allow the Germans to take them away.

Hungarian Jews, primarily women and children, arriving at Auschwitz.

Two days later, four German Army divisions arrived in Budapest. That night, September 10, the German Police Prison was raided.

"All the lights were suddenly turned on," Catherine wrote. "Moaning, weeping and screams slashed the stillness of the early morning. We listened in terror, and learned that most of the Polish prisoners were being rounded up for deportation. I had heard of the 'night roundups,' but had never before witnessed one. Our door was opened by a soldier who read off the name of the unfortunate woman from Krakow. He left the door open and we could see the group of victims in the corridor, wailing and sobbing."

Catherine was later told that Hannah "fell on the bed and sobbed" when the Gestapo took four of her cellmates away. "Those who remained were surprised, considering [Hannah's] usual moral strength and courage," Catherine wrote. Hannah soon "pulled herself together," however, and was once more "the one to instill hope in the others."

The next morning, a young prisoner working in the corridor called Catherine to the door and told her "the sickening news": Hannah herself had just been taken away. She was gone, no one knew where. "I was destroyed," Catherine wrote, "my world at an end."

Yoel Palgi was taken from the German Police Prison on the same day and driven off in the same prison van. Along with several others, he and Hannah were taken to the Hungarian Army Prison, where they spent the night talking about all that had happened since they were last together. "Happiness and deep sorrow were mingled in our talk," Palgi later wrote. The next day they were taken back to the prison van. This time, at its first stop, Hannah alone was led off. Yoel watched from the window. "She stood at the gate looking so young, so brave," he wrote later. "As the van moved off, she put down her bag and gave us an encouraging thumbs up sign, her lovely face wreathed in a smile."

CHAPTER 13

OCTOBER

"Save my people in the short time it remains in your power to do so"

TWO days after Hannah was taken away, almost all the prisoners at the German Police Prison were ordered into the yard. There they were told that they were being transferred to Kistarcsa. Rumors flew. Were the Germans getting ready to flee? Some prisoners were jubilant, but Catherine was beside herself with anxiety over Hannah. As she was being herded across the yard to the waiting buses, she broke out of the line to ask an official she recognized "where they had taken Hannah." The man assured her he had no idea. But perhaps because of Catherine's extreme distress, he added that he "imagined it would be a better place." Catherine moved on.

When the prisoners arrived at the internment camp, they found an enormous crowd awaiting them. "We gazed at one another," Catherine wrote, "our eyes seeking familiar faces." She saw several people she knew, but not Hannah. "There were many bitter disappointments."

The rules at Kistarcsa were very relaxed. Compared to the German Police Prison, the camp seemed to Catherine to be almost like a summer resort. Prisoners were allowed to walk about freely, to write as many letters as they liked. Some were even allowed to have visitors.

"Tormented by worry about Hannah," Catherine wrote to Margit and to her sister, begging them to try to locate her. But they could learn nothing. Then, on Yom Kippur, two weeks after Catherine's arrival at Kistarcsa, it was suddenly announced that the camp was closing. One by one, the prisoners' names were called and they were released.

It was late afternoon, the September sun was already setting, when Catherine made her way to her sister's home, a Yellow Star house on Alkotmány Street. Catherine was wearier than she could ever remember being. How would she find Hannah? What would happen to her? Who would help her?

Slowly she climbed the steps to her sister's front door and knocked. "She could hardly believe her eyes when she saw me," she wrote later, "and I, for my part, was shocked by my sister's appearance. Worry and constant running from place to place in futile attempts to find Hannah and to effect my release had changed her into a prematurely aged, care-worn matron."

But there was very good news. Hannah had been found. A young Hungarian lawyer named Nánay had contacted Catherine's sister just the day before. He had visited Hannah in prison, he said, and had offered to defend her. She had asked him to contact her family.

Catherine and her brother-in-law (also a lawyer) went to see Dr. Nánay the next day. The young lawyer told them that he was defending two other parachutists from Palestine, Yoel Palgi and Peretz Goldstein. They were being held at the Margit Boulevard Prison. It was Palgi and Goldstein who had told Nánay that Hannah was at the Conti Street Prison and asked him to visit her there. Nánay was willing to prepare a defense for all of them, but Catherine wanted to consult her "friend and family counselor," a Dr. Palágyi, before making any decision about how best to handle Hannah's case. Above all, she wanted to talk to Hannah herself, and ask her what she wanted her to do. Dr. Nánay understood Catherine's feelings, and promised to get her a visitor's pass to the Conti Street Prison as soon as possible.

On the way back to her sister's house, Catherine stopped at her own home to tell Margit all that had happened. Margit had news of her own. Two men had visited her dressing room the night before and given her an envelope that they said was from "someone named Geri." They asked her to give it to Hannah so that she would lack "for nothing in prison." Catherine opened the envelope. There was a "considerable sum" of money inside. "Of course, at the time," Catherine wrote, "I had no idea who the mysterious Geri was, but later discovered he was Reuven Dafne, her parachutist comrade who had been with her in Yugoslavia among the partisans."

Catherine left, feeling more hopeful than she had felt in months.

Several days later, October 6, the Russian Army broke into southern Hungary. Advance forces were said to be only 100 miles from Budapest. Dr. Nánay was full of cheerful speculation about the end of the war as he accompanied Catherine to the Conti Street Prison. She was allowed ten minutes with Hannah, who was flanked by two guards. "She looked remarkably well," Catherine later wrote. And although they couldn't quite speak freely in front of the guards, "at least we could embrace."

First Catherine gave Hannah the parcel she had prepared for her. Although there were severe food shortages in Budapest, when friends and relatives heard that Catherine was going to visit her daughter, "they had hurriedly brought whatever they could," Catherine wrote, "including items of clothing and other odds and ends they thought might please her."

Catherine herself had unearthed a sewing set Hannah had received as a child and included it in the parcel. "As an experienced ex-prisoner," she wrote, "I knew the importance of such a thing." Everything in the package delighted Hannah, but the sewing set above all. "It brought tears to her eyes, and she asked: 'Does this thing still exist? Was there ever such a time . . . a time of childhood and carefree happiness?'" Then Catherine gave Hannah greetings from Geri. "Her eyes sparkled and she beamed."

At Catherine's questioning, Hannah said that she would also like to have some books, "as many as you can send. Reading is allowed here. . . . More than anything else," she added, "I'd like a Bible. A Hebrew Bible." She also admitted that it was sometimes quite cold in the cell, and asked her mother to bring her some warmer clothing. Except for that, she said, everything was fine. She was not in solitary confinement, and the prisoners with whom she shared a cell were "young, spirited, and optimistic." "Actually," Catherine wrote, "during all the months she was imprisoned, I never heard her complain about anything."

Years later, Catherine met one of Hannah's Conti Street cellmates. The woman recalled how Hannah had "won their hearts" in the short time they had been together. She had introduced herself to them as a Zionist, and since "they did not know exactly what 'Zionist' meant . . . they were suspicious and kept away from her at first." However, they soon realized that Hannah "was helpful to all of them, and . . . shared with them or gave them whatever she had. . . . Soon the barrier between them was torn down, and they all felt her warmth and kind-heartedness."

Just before Catherine left Hannah told her she was going to be tried soon and needed a lawyer. "Decide on someone as soon as possible," she said to her mother.

Back at her sister's house, Catherine was inundated with advice from friends and relatives on how best to aid her daughter. Most people urged her to contact the Zionist Organization and ask someone there to help. Catherine did, and was directed to a young man, a Mr. Grossman, who assured her that he already knew about the case of the young Palestinian parachutists and that "everything possible" was being done for them. "But in the course of our relatively brief conversation," Catherine wrote, "it transpired that he didn't even know Hannah had already been in the Conti Street Prison for nearly three weeks. He thought she was in the Margit Boulevard Prison, along with her comrades."

Nevertheless, he urged Catherine not to worry and assured her that everything was under control.

Catherine tried to believe that Grossman knew what he was doing. She returned to his office early the next morning, to see whether he had learned anything more, and to find out exactly what was being done for her daughter. Again Grossman told her not to worry and promised that "everything possible was being done."

Catherine returned again the following morning, and the morning after that. "Every day I worried because I had not found a lawyer, but Grossman said there was no need, everything was already arranged. . . . He said it [getting a lawyer] wasn't necessary because Hannah would be let out of prison the next day, or the day after, or maybe even the same day." Catherine asked for the name of a lawyer who could at least get a package through to Hannah. "Hannah was cold," Catherine recalled telling Grossman, "and had no dresses with her, and she had asked me at the beginning of October to send her some warm things and food."

Grossman said she didn't need a lawyer for that. His superior, Rezsö Kastner, head of the Zionist Organization, had the right to go into the prison. "If that's the case," Catherine said, "why doesn't he go? Is it possible to speak to him?" Catherine asked for Kastner's home address, but Grossman said he could not give it to her. She learned it, in spite of him, from one of her acquaintances and went directly there.

"The gatekeeper told me that Kastner used to live there, but had moved. He gave me the number of another apartment where a family lived that was friendly with Kastner. I went up there and rang the bell. A woman looked out the window. At first she didn't want to let me in. I said to her that this was a very pressing Zionist matter. I told her my name, and that from what I had heard Kastner was the only man who could help me. There were parachutists here from Palestine, and my daughter was one of them, and I had heard that Kastner had the right to visit them in prison. The woman said they knew about it, and Kastner really intended to visit the prison. She thought he would be going there tomorrow, and it would be a good idea for me to get a package ready." She told Catherine to go directly to Kastner's office, and that his secretary would arrange things.

The next day, Catherine went to Kastner's office, but the secretary told her Kastner was not in and would not be going to the prison that day. So Catherine returned the following day, but the secretary said Kastner would not be in that day either. Catherine went to the office, as she later recalled, "at least three times, perhaps four. Kastner was never there, only his secretary. She said he hadn't come in yet. Nor did they take the package from me."

On October 12, Catherine once again returned to Kastner's office. This time the secretary told her to wait. Perhaps Kastner would come in soon. Several other people were waiting in the office too. One of them told Catherine that Otto Komoly, another well-known and well-connected official of the Zionist Organization was in the building at that moment.

"Komoly knew our family," Catherine wrote, "and he knew Hannah. I went to him and asked him to tell me the whole truth about Hannah, for every day they promised me they'd take care of everything, that there was no point in getting a lawyer.

"He stared at me and said, 'What, Hannah here?'

"I said to him: 'How is it you don't know that some emissaries have come from Palestine, some boys and Hannah?'

"Then Komoly said that was the first he'd heard that Hannah was one of the group. And he added: 'I assure you we shall do everything in our power. Meanwhile get yourself a lawyer at once, this very day.'"

Catherine's head was spinning. Weeks before she had asked her friend Dr. Palágyi to examine the list of defense lawyers available and to tell her the one he thought the very best. Dr. Palágyi had named a Dr. Szelecsényi, who had recently won a series of complicated cases. Now, Catherine called Dr. Palágyi. With him, she visited Dr. Szelecsényi and entrusted him with Hannah's defense. "He promised he would see her in prison the next day, and that he would make every effort to obtain a pass for me to visit her."

Meanwhile Catherine searched for a Hebrew Bible for Hannah. All the book shops dealing in Jewish or Hebrew literature had been closed months before. She called at the home of the former owner of the largest Jewish bookstore in Budapest, but he had fled the country. In the best-known Christian-owned religious book store, Catherine's request was greeted with surprise. They had the Bible in all languages, the clerk said, "but certainly not" in Hebrew. "To my everlasting sorrow," Catherine wrote, "I was unable to fulfill Hannah's last wish."

Dr. Szelecsényi was on his way to visit Hannah in prison on the thirteenth of October when a massive Allied air raid began that drove everyone to the shelters. The air raid lasted for hours, so it was Saturday, the fourteenth, before he saw Hannah and heard her full story. Later he said to Catherine that "he doubted whether one man in a thousand would have undertaken and accomplished the things Hannah had." If her case went to trial, he thought she would certainly be convicted. She might even be sentenced to as many as five or six years. However it didn't really matter what the sentence was, he said, for at the end of the war all political prisoners would be released immediately. "And I don't need to tell you how the war stands now," he added. "There is absolutely no possibility of a death sentence. I'm not saying this just to calm your fears, but because that is my sincere conviction."

Early the next morning, the fifteenth of October, the Twenty-fourth German Panzer Division, with forty tanks, rolled into Budapest in a surprise move that stunned everyone. Its orders were to depose the Horthy-Lakatos regime. At 10 A.M., two hours before Horthy was scheduled to broadcast an appeal to the Russians and the Allies for an armistice, the Germans kidnapped his son. Veesenmayer himself delivered the ultimatum: at the least sign of treason—which an appeal for an armistice would certainly be—Horthy's son would be killed. At this, the old Regent broke down and cried. He cancelled the broadcast and the next day, October 16, surrendered himself to the Germans. Prime Minister Lakatos surrendered also. Both men were sent to prison in Germany.

Arrow Cross leader Ferenc Szálasi took control of the Hungarian government, eager to do Hitler's bidding with the zeal of a true believer. Eichmann himself returned to Budapest on October 17 and joined forces with Szálasi. The interrupted roundups were to be resumed immediately.

There was a desperate shortage of workers in Germany by this time, and the Nazis were, as Nora Levin put it, "scraping at the remnants" of living Jews in all the occupied countries in order to staff their factories. Eichmann decided to send the Jews of

Jewish labor brigade after an air raid.

Budapest, the last remaining Jews in Hungary, to Germany as slaves. Since most railroad lines in Hungary had been bombed, Eichmann planned to have them walk the 120 miles to the Austrian border. Although the war was almost over, a gruesome last-minute nightmare was just beginning for Hungarian Jews.

This murderous scheme was only one of several furious actions that Hitler ordered during the last months of the war. The fact that the Nazis were losing ground on every front, combined with an attempt to assassinate him in late July, had driven Hitler into a frenzy. He saw conspirators everywhere and seemed possessed by a wild determination to do as much as possible in the little time left before Germany was defeated. "Half-mad, deteriorating in mind and body, Hitler whipped beaten armies, demoralized generals and a bomb-dazed nation to a final effort that prolonged for almost a year the agony of a war that Germany had already lost," wrote Levin. "The war to exterminate European Jewry was still very much part of that war."

On October 20, three days after Eichmann's return, the roundups of Hungarian Jews began again. Szálasi's Arrow Cross men, under Eichmann's direction, began knocking on the doors of Yellow Star houses, seizing all men between the ages of sixteen and sixty. As heavy rains fell, those arrested were made to run along the streets and thoroughfares to the center of the city. As their numbers increased they looked, according to one observer, like "crazed ants." On that first day, 22,000 men were rounded up. The following day, the drive was extended to include women. By the end of the week, 35,000 Jews had been seized. And the roundups continued.

The nightmare timing of these events left Catherine numb with terror for her daughter. Virtually housebound now, since Jews were permitted on the streets only for two hours a day and only on certain days, she could not visit the prison, or Dr. Szelecsényi. Jews had long since been deprived of private phones and were not allowed to use public phones, so Catherine could not even consult with the lawyer about the defense he was preparing. Through her sister and her husband (who were under Swedish protection and didn't have to wear the Yellow Star), she learned that Hannah's trial would be held on the twenty-eighth and reached Szelecsényi from the telephone of a Christian friend. To her "desperate question" as to what would happen to Hannah now, "in view of the changed political situation," Szelecsényi replied: "It is possible that her sentence will be ten or twenty years, maybe even life. However, that does not essentially change matters." Hannah would be freed in any case when the war was over, he said. And he still believed it would be over soon.

On October 28, despite the dangers, Catherine made her way to the Margit Boulevard Prison where Hannah's trial was to be held. "Those were the times when Jews were not allowed on the street," Yoel Palgi wrote later, "but she, the mother, had come."

Not allowed to enter the courtroom, Catherine waited in the antechamber near a sign that read: "Hannah Senesh and Accomplices."

The records of Hannah's trial were destroyed sometime afterward by the officials in charge. But we know most of what went on because Fleishmann and Tissandier, Hannah's "accomplices," were present almost the entire time and later put together a reconstruction of it. Hannah was first asked to state whether she was guilty or not guilty, and then she was given an opportunity to speak on her own behalf. According to Fleishmann and Tissandier, she opened with an account of the roots of her beliefs.

"I was born in Budapest," she began. "Here I learned to love the beautiful, to honor my neighbor and respect the good. The Hungarians were a beaten and suffering people. Through my love for them I learned to understand the beaten and the suffering. I dreamed of a beautiful world, which would be compassionate toward Hungarians because of their suffering. I thought we would be able to repay the world for its compassion with what we had learned: an understanding for all the suffering people of the world, and a desire to help the weak."

She spoke about her father, saying he had been an example to her of "working for the sake of goodness" and that he had taught her "to have faith in the good." As a child she had believed that the "spiritual Hungary" she absorbed from reading the Hungarian classics was the "true Hungary." "But when I grew up the streets of the city taught me that as a Jewess I had no place in this country. One by one, the politicians voted for race discrimination, deprivation of human rights, the cruelty of the Middle Ages. Farmers in the villages were hungry for bread and threatened the landowners who, instead of dividing their surplus crops, threw them the Jews, history's scapegoat. I awakened from my dream, the dream of my father and my father's father. I understood then that I have no Homeland. You cancelled my citizenship with your hate. I went away to build a Homeland, a Homeland of my own, a Jewish Homeland, a true Homeland."

Hannah condemned the government that had led Hungary into the war "unnecessarily, without justification . . . and on the side of evil." At this there were shouts for Hannah to be silenced, but the President of the Tribunal allowed her to continue. "You joined forces with our blood enemies—the Germans," Hannah said. "And thus you became my enemy. But even that was not enough for me to come and fight against you. I still clung to the love of my youth. I was sorry for the Hungarian people who were always so close to my heart, who had fallen victim of their conscienceless leaders. And that was still not enough for you. You also raised your hand against my people. Thus," she concluded, "it is not I who is the traitor! They are the traitors who brought this calamity upon our people, and upon themselves! I implore you," Hannah said, "don't add to your crimes. Save my people in the short time it remains in your power to do so. Every Jew who remains alive in Hungary will make the judgment against you after you fall."

At eleven o'clock, the judges retired to deliberate and the doors of the courtroom were thrown open. "I glimpsed Hannah amidst the group streaming out," Catherine wrote. "She had no idea I would be there, and rushing over, threw her arms around me. The guard separated us, and said he could permit us to talk only after sentence had been passed. . . . She [Hannah] was flushed," Catherine recalled, "excited, her eyes brilliant, her smile self-confident."

Soon Hannah was called back into the courtroom, but in a few minutes, she came out again. The judges had not been able to reach a decision! Instead, they had announced that sentencing was being postponed for eight days, until Saturday, November 4. Catherine was frightened, but Dr. Szelecsényi said that the delay had no significance. Hannah herself was confident. "Why worry about a sentence when we'll all soon be free."

Dr. Szelecsényi had to rush off to another trial and Hannah thanked him for a "brilliant defense." The lawyer, who had been attacked by members of the court for agreeing to defend the "Jew girl," was very pleased with Hannah's praise. Then, advising Catherine and Hannah to make the most of the few moments they would have together now, he left.

Catherine could not hide her anxiety and Hannah tried to reassure her. The delay made no difference, she said, because she would not be released from prison anyway as long as the war continued. "But I'm astonished that you walk about the streets so freely," she said to Catherine. "Why don't you disappear? What about your Gentile friends? Can't they hide you?"

Catherine said she wouldn't even think about hiding until Hannah's case was settled. Hannah replied, "I'll muddle through this somehow, believe me. But I won't have a moment's peace as long as you're so careless."

Hannah's guard came to take Hannah away. However, he said pleasantly that since the trial was over, Catherine would be allowed to visit her daughter in the Conti Street Prison at any time. The three of them went down the stairs together, but at the bottom, Catherine was stopped.

"I was not allowed to walk across the yard with them," Catherine wrote, "so [I] watched her walk away until she disappeared from view, lost in the mob."

CHAPTER 14

NOVEMBER

"Wonderful, sparkling Hannah"

O N October 30 and again on October 31, Budapest was bombed by Allied bombers. The air raids were so intense Catherine could not leave the house, and so she could not get to the Conti Street Prison to visit Hannah.

On November 1, she made it to the prison, only to discover that because it was a religious holiday—All Saints Day—visitors were not permitted.

On November 2, she returned and was told that since sentence on Hannah had not yet been passed, she would have to get special permission to visit her daughter from Captain Simon, who had been the Judge Advocate at the trial. His office was not at the Conti Street Prison, but at the Hadik Military Barracks on the other side of town. Catherine did not have time to go directly there because Jews were allowed on the street for only two hours a day, from ten until noon. She went there the next day, November 3, only to be told that the Judge Advocate was out of town and would not be back for four days. Beside herself, Catherine said that her daughter was supposed to be sentenced the following

The Budapest Chain Bridge destroyed.

day—November 4. There must be someone who could give her a visitor's pass. The clerk insisted, however, that no one had been assigned to replace Captain Simon during his absence, and no one was authorized to issue passes while he was away.

To Catherine's increasing confusion, Dr. Szelecsényi added the fact that the date for passing sentence on Hannah had been postponed once again. Also, that Captain Simon had been taken off the case. A new Judge Advocate was going to be appointed "soon." He promised to let Catherine know "without an instant's delay" as soon as he learned who the new Judge Advocate was to be and as soon as a new date for sentencing was set. He urged her to remain calm.

Those were the days when "confusion reigned," Yoel Palgi wrote, recalling that autumn in prison. Rumors and speculations were passed from prisoner to prisoner about the progress of the Russian Army, when and how it would enter Budapest, what would happen when it did. One by one, judges and other officials of the German regime disappeared, and everyone knew they had fled the city. "Prison boilers became pyres for court records," Yoel wrote. "Artillery thunder increased hourly until our window panes rattled."

The Conti Street Prison was evacuated. Hannah was transferred to the Margit Boulevard Prison, where Yoel Palgi was being held. There were rumors that the Margit Boulevard Prison was going to be evacuated too, and the prisoners transferred to sites west of Budapest, out of the line of the advancing Russian Army. "We had two fervent wishes," Yoel wrote, "that they would not move us before the Russians arrived, and that they would bring us food. We suffered desperately from hunger. Because of the frequent bombardments we were sometimes given soup only once a day, and in the penetrating cold of late autumn we trembled with hunger and increasing weakness. It sometimes seemed that even if we were lucky enough not to be moved, we would starve to death before the Red Army broke through."

On the fourth, fifth and sixth of November, Catherine stayed at home, waiting to hear from Dr. Szelencsényi, trying to remain calm. There were air raids during the day; at night, guns could be heard in the distance.

Early on the morning of November 7, the day she had been told Captain Simon would return, Catherine set out once again for Hadik Military Barracks. She had with her a letter from Dr. Szelencsényi that explained that a date for sentencing had not yet been passed and that a new Judge Advocate had not yet been named. Captain Simon was, therefore, still the only one who could give Catherine permission to visit Hannah.

Catherine found the Hadik Barracks in "total confusion." One crammed moving van after another was pulling out. At the main building, the doorman told her it was pointless to enter since "as far as he knew everyone was already gone." "Certainly the roar of the Russian guns was increasing even as we talked," Catherine recalled. "The mass flight of the Fascists to the West had begun."

Nevertheless, Catherine insisted upon going to Captain Simon's office "on the chance that he might still be there." After "a great deal of persuasion," the doorman allowed her to go inside. "There everything had indeed been packed," she wrote, "but I found two female clerks in hats and coats, and a young officer. All were on the point of leaving. The officer was the one I had talked to on my last visit there, when Captain Simon was out of town. So I explained once again that I still desperately wanted the visitor's permit. The officer answered that Simon had been transferred the previous day to Margit Boulevard Military Prison, and gave me the number of the Captain's office there. Then, glancing at his watch, he added, 'You had better hurry.' I understood this last to mean the Captain would soon be leaving his office and that if I wanted to catch him I should move fast."

Catherine arrived at the Margit Boulevard Prison at about ten-thirty. "It was quiet and comparatively deserted," she wrote. "From the sentry at the entrance [of the prison] to the Captain's office, I did not pass a soul, and had the impression everyone had fled the building. After wandering up and down the corridors of the seemingly deserted building, I found the right office. It was empty, but a briefcase on one of the desks, with a pair of gloves resting on it, indicated that its owner was still in the building. I waited in the corridor. A clerk appeared, who confirmed that Captain Simon was still there."

The timing of events on that cloudy November 7 was so close as to seem impossible. Yet it was less than two hours before Catherine's arrival at the Margit Boulevard Prison that Captain Simon decided to take the case of Hannah Senesh into his own hands. His superiors had fled the day before without passing sentence. He himself had burned all the records pertaining to her case and many others. His files had been packed into cartons, his desk was empty and he was ready to leave. Then he decided to perform this last "official" act. We will never know why. But according to the eyewitness account of a prisoner on cleaning duty outside Hannah's cell, Captain Simon entered the cell just before nine A.M. and said:

"Hannah Senesh, you have been sentenced to death. Do you wish to ask for clemency?"

"Sentenced to death?" Hannah said. "No, I wish to appeal. Bring in my lawyer."

"You cannot appeal," Simon said. "You may ask for clemency."

"I was tried before a lower tribunal. I know I have the right to appeal."

"There are no appeals," Simon repeated. "Do you or do you not wish to ask for clemency?"

"Clemency—from you? Do you think I'm going to plead with hangmen and murderers? I shall never ask you for mercy."

"In that case, prepare to die!" Simon said. "You may write farewell letters. But hurry. We shall carry out the sentence in one hour from now."

Hannah sat motionless in her cell, her eyes fixed to a point on the wall. "What she saw there," Yoel wrote later, "what she was staring at, we shall never know. Perhaps her mother's face, perhaps the scenes of her childhood—the sea, the places and the people so dear to her." Paper and pen were brought to Hannah and she wrote letters. No one besides Simon ever saw them, for he destroyed them.

At ten A.M., the prisoner recounted, Captain Simon returned to Hannah's cell and silently signaled her to follow him. She rose immediately and walked behind him. Two soldiers fell into step beside her and "escorted" her to the courtyard. The prisoner watched from the window.

"Next to the gray brick wall, near the little prison church, stood a wooden sandbox," the prisoner later told Yoel. "They [the soldiers] drove a post into the sand, tied her hands behind her back, and strapped her to it. Hannah observed all the gloomy preparations with wonder. She looked straight into the eyes of the officer, who stepped toward her with a blindfold. She shook her head defiantly and lifted her blue eyes to the cloudy, foreboding sky."

Three rifles fired. Hannah was dead.

In their cell on the second floor, Yoel Palgi and his cellmates heard the shots.

"We looked at each other, frightened and bewildered," he wrote later. "What had happened? Had someone been executed? Impossible! That was not their method. Last respects were always paid. There was always the marching of the firing squad, the reading of the sentence, prayer and a bugle call accompanying the dark moment of execution in the gray courtyard beneath our cell window. Someone climbed up to the high window, and looking down informed us that he could see a table with a crucifix on it, but no sign of an execution. At the same moment we heard voices in the courtyard—an order to rearrange the straw. Apparently a guard had fired a bullet by accident and the reverberation had amplified the sound."

At eleven forty-five, Captain Simon returned to his office where Catherine Senesh had been waiting since ten-thirty.

"I . . . introduced myself," she wrote, "and asked for a visitor's pass.

"The case no longer has anything to do with me," he answered briskly. Catherine thought he looked ill at ease.

"Then who is in charge of the case?" she asked.

"I don't know," Simon said.

"Who is authorized to grant me a visitor's permit?"

"I don't know," he said again.

"His brusque, summary answers released all my bitterness," Catherine wrote. She remembered saying, " 'Captain, at least be helpful enough to direct me to the proper authorities, and tell me what I must do in order to see my daughter. As it is, I can't understand why it's so difficult for me to obtain a pass when relatives of other prisoners have been permitted frequent visiting rights. I have been granted permission to see my daughter only once, and then only for a minute.' "

"Really?" Captain Simon said. "I didn't grant you even once permission to see her!"

"And how is it possible that there still has not been a date set for sentencing?" Catherine continued. "The eight-day postponement has long since expired." Simon did not answer, and Catherine went on. "Or has sentence been passed?"

"Even if it has been," Captain Simon said, "I'm not in a position to tell you what it entails."

Catherine was beside herself. "What do you mean?" she asked. "You don't mean to tell me it would be possible to keep such information from me?"

He did not reply. Catherine repeated: "*Has* sentence been passed?"

"Captain Simon then went to his desk," Catherine wrote, "sat down, pointed to the chair opposite. 'Sit down.' Finally he said, 'Do you know what your daughter's case is about?' "

"Yes," Catherine said. "The lawyer has briefed me."

Ignoring this answer, he summarized the case.

"Your daughter, after renouncing her Hungarian citizenship, joined the British Armed Forces and was a Radio Officer in the Parachute Corps. Last spring she flew from Cairo, via Italy, to Yugoslavia, where she was dropped and spent a considerable length of time with the partisans. From Yugoslavia she made her way to Hungary, supposedly for the purpose of rescuing Jews and

British prisoners of war. In other words, she is guilty of major crimes against the interests of Hungary."

"That isn't true," Catherine interrupted. "When we met in the Gestapo [German Police] prison yard, I questioned her about her mission. She said she could not answer my questions because she was bound by military secrecy; but she assured me she had positively not undertaken . . . any act which could possibly be detrimental to the welfare of Hungary. On the contrary!"

"But Hungary is under martial law," Simon said, "and your daughter was found with a radio transmitter. Consequently the Military Tribunal found her guilty of treason, and demanded the supreme penalty. And this . . . penalty . . . has already been . . . carried out."

"I looked at him, petrified," Catherine wrote. "The world went black."

Suddenly she remembered the letter she had received from Dr. Szelecsényi that stated that sentence had not been passed. "Perhaps this man was merely deriving some form of brutal pleasure in torturing me," she wrote. "I clung to this thought as a last straw, and finally said, 'No, no. That's impossible. It can't be. Why . . . I received a letter from the lawyer telling me sentence had not yet been passed, and that he would let me know when the day was fixed for sentencing. Certainly the lawyer would have been informed if anything had happened.'

"Yes, of course," Captain Simon said. "He knows, but probably wants to spare you."

"Spare me? What sense would that make? How long do you suppose I would be spared? No. The lawyer must have told me the truth."

"What's the name of the lawyer?" Simon asked.

Catherine gave him Dr. Szelecsényi's letter. Simon examined it, made a note of the lawyer's name and telephone number, and said, "All right, we'll inform him by phone."

There was no hope left. "And this is the way it happens?" Catherine stammered. "Such things exist? They can really happen? And I wasn't even allowed to see her, to talk to her."

—190—

"She didn't want to see you," Simon said. "She wanted to spare you the shock." Later, he told Dr. Szelecsényi just the opposite: Hannah did indeed ask to see Catherine. It was her last request, but it was refused. "But you'll be given farewell letters," Simon added. "She wrote several." He said Catherine could pick them up at the Conti Street Prison.

"As I staggered down the stairs, unseeing," Catherine wrote, "it suddenly struck me that Simon had just come from the execution."

That afternoon, one of Yoel's cellmates returned from the prison infirmary shaken and pale. "He leaned against the wall for support," Yoel later wrote, "and announced in a faint voice, 'They've executed Hannah. That was the firing we heard.'"

Yoel did not believe him. "After the first wave of shock," he recalled, "I became convinced that it was an error, that my cellmate had misunderstood." Pounding on the cell door, Yoel yelled until a guard came. "We want to know who was just executed," he cried.

"Don't worry, she wasn't one of yours," the guard finally said. "Just some young girl . . . a partisan, they say . . . a British parachutist. But that's surely a lie. Whoever heard of a young girl being a British officer?"

"So it was Hannah after all," Yoel wrote. "Wonderful, sparkling Hannah. She was the first to go. She, who had been so sure we would return to tell our comrades of our exploits, to spin tall tales. I felt I had to speak, but the words strangled in my throat . . .

"We rose and stood in silence for a long while, honoring her memory the only way we could. Then we just sat down, speechless, stunned. Tears would not come. I couldn't find anything to say. All I could hear were my cellmate's words over and over again: 'They executed Hannah . . .'"

Several days later, Catherine and her sister went to the Conti Street Prison for Hannah's letters. Officials gave Catherine the last of Hannah's belongings, but there were no letters among them. They advised her to return to the Margit Boulevard Prison and

The Margit Boulevard Prison where Hannah Senesh was executed.

check again with Captain Simon. By the time Catherine returned to Margit Boulevard, Captain Simon was gone, the letters with him. But in the pocket of one of the dresses the warden at Conti Street had given her, Catherine found a note. It was not dated, but it was written to her. It was a note of farewell.

Dearest Mother:

I don't know what to say—only this:
a million thanks, and forgive me, if you can.
You know so well why words aren't
necessary. With love forever,

Your daughter

PART THREE

1945 and After

CHAPTER 15

1945

"Never say that there is only death for you"

IN February 1945, three months after Hannah was killed, the Russian Army took control of Budapest and ousted the Arrow Cross government. For Hungary, the war was over. Five hundred and fifty thousand Jews, seventy percent of all the Jews in greater Hungary, had perished in the nine months of Nazi rule. Catherine Senesh herself had been caught in one of Eichmann's roundups and forced on what was called The Long March. When the soldiers came to get her, she did not resist. "I was totally indifferent," she wrote. "A week after my Hannah was murdered, this appeared to me to be a fitting solution."

In May 1945, six months after Hannah's death, Germany surrendered to the Allies. Hitler, fifty feet below the earth in a bunker-fortress outside Berlin, committed suicide. The war in Europe was over. Five million Jewish adults and one and a half million Jewish children had been murdered since the German onslaught began.

Throughout the summer and fall that followed, accounts of

Elderly Jews of Budapest being rounded up for the Long March.

the grisly death camps poured out of Europe, stunning and horrifying the world. The soldiers who were the first to see the inmates were said to have been "shattered." A word was coined to describe some of the survivors: *musselmen,* people who were neither living nor dead. "Kindness itself had not the power to make them speak," one observer said. "They would only look at you with a long expressionless stare. If they tried to answer, the tongues could not reach their dried up palates to make a sound. One was aware only of a poisonous breath rising out of entrails already in a state of decomposition."

The attempt to destroy the Jews of Europe came to be called the Holocaust, the "great destruction and devastation."* But the things the Nazis had done seemed beyond the power of words to describe or explain. Almost as bewildering, when it came to light, was the Allied governments' failure to even attempt to

---

*The word holocaust has its root in the Hebrew *olah,* which means: a burnt offering, an offering made by fire to the Lord. It made its way into English through the Greek *holokauston:* a sacrifice or offering wholly consumed by fire. Holocaust is the word Jews have chosen to name their experience in Nazi Europe.

rescue the Jews of Europe, despite the fact that, unlike the civilian populations, they had known about the Nazis' plans almost from the beginning.

"We knew in Washington, from August 1942 on, that the Nazis were planning to exterminate all the Jews of Europe," wrote Secretary of the United States Treasury, Henry Morgenthau, Jr. "Yet . . . the State Department did practically nothing. Officials dodged their grim responsibility, procrastinated when concrete rescue schemes were placed before them, and even suppressed information about atrocities in order to prevent an outraged public opinion from forcing their hand."

In October 1942, Jan Karski, liaison officer between the Polish government-in-exile in London and the Polish underground, met with leaders of the Jewish underground in Warsaw. They were "unforgettable," Karski wrote, "less like men than incarnations of mass suffering and nerves strained in hopeless effort. . . . It was an evening of nightmare."

Karski urged the men to speak frankly. "I will be in London soon," he said, "and in a position to obtain audiences with the Allied authorities. . . . My status will be official and you must give me your official message to the outside world. You are the leaders of the Jewish underground. What do you want me to say?"

"We want you to tell the Polish and Allied governments" one of the men said, "that we are helpless in the face of the German criminals. We cannot defend ourselves and no one in Poland can defend us. The Germans are not trying to enslave us as they have other people; we are being systematically murdered. . . . three million Polish Jews are doomed. . . . Place this responsibility on the shoulders of the Allies. Let not a single leader be able to say that they did not know that we were being murdered in Poland and could not be helped except from the outside."

Before returning to London, Karski visited the Warsaw ghetto for himself. "To pass that wall was to enter a new world utterly unlike anything that had ever been imagined," he reported. ". . . Everywhere there was hunger, misery, the atrocious stench of decomposing bodies, the pitiful moan of dying children, the desperate cries and gasps of a people struggling for life against impossible odds. . . . Everyone and everything seemed to vibrate with unnatural intensity, to be in constant motion, enveloped in a haze of disease and death through which their bodies appeared to be throbbing in disintegration." Karski fled the ghetto in horror, reluctant even to breathe the air.

In November, he reported what he had heard and seen to the Polish government-in-exile, to members of the British government, the American government, and to Jewish leaders. Later in the month, the eyewitness description of Treblinka death camp reached the West, along with a plea for weapons and support from the Jewish Fighting Organization in the Warsaw ghetto. Help was not forthcoming from any quarter.

In December, the Polish government-in-exile issued a paper called "The Mass Extermination of Jews in German-Occupied Poland," and in response, the United States, Great Britain and the Soviet Union issued a "Declaration of Solemn Protest," pledging that those responsible would not escape "retribution" when the war was over. But no Allied government devised any plan or attempted any direct action to aid the Jews. Nor had any government ever done so. When it had been possible to bring Jews out of Germany by paying money to the German government, the Allies ignored or turned down large-scale ransom schemes and strategies. Later, the Allied Air Command ignored or turned down requests to bomb the death camps and the railroad lines leading to them, although from a military point of view it would have been possible to do so. Munitions factories a few miles from Auschwitz were destroyed by Allied bombers, and fires from the crematoria burned night and day and were visible for miles, making perfect targets, but they were never bombed.

In the spring of 1943, Shmuel Artur Zygelboym, Polish Jew and member of the Polish National Council in London, who had tried desperately to rally help for the Jews of Poland and particularly the Jews of Warsaw before and during the uprising, killed himself in an agony of sorrow and protest against the silence that had greeted his pleas. This is the farewell letter he left:

> "I cannot be silent. I cannot live while the remnants of the Jewish population of Poland, of whom I am a representative, are perishing. My friends in the Warsaw ghetto died with weapons in their hands in the last heroic battle. It was not my destiny to die together with them, but I belong to them and in their mass graves.
>
> "By my death I wish to make my final protest against the passivity with which the world is looking on and permitting the extermination of the Jewish people. I know how little human life is worth today, but as I was unable to do anything during my lifetime, perhaps by my death I shall contribute to breaking down the indifference of those who may now at the last moment rescue the few Polish Jews still alive."

The destruction of the Jews was a major goal of the war for Germany. Their rescue was not a major wartime goal for the Allies. The Jews of Europe had been left to face the Nazis alone.

Accounts of Jewish resistance were a long time coming to the fore. Even today the full story is not widely known, and many people continue to believe that the Jews did not resist at all, that in fact they willingly assisted in their own destruction. "Nothing could be further from the truth," writes Yuri Suhl, a chronicler of Jewish resistance in Europe. "Jewish resistance to the Nazis constitutes a glorious chapter in the history of human courage," writes Irving J. Rosenbaum, student of Judaism and of the Holocaust. "Rarely have women and men demonstrated so much bravery in the face of such hopelessness." The earliest accounts of the Holocaust were ignorant of the Jewish resistance because they were based almost entirely on captured German documents —over 15,000,000 official pages describing the Nazi regime and its operations, which the Allies made available to historians and other scholars after the war. As Lucy Dawidowicz, a leading scholar of the Holocaust, points out, the researchers who pored through these records found a great deal of information about the German program to destroy the Jews, but very little about what the Jews did to defend themselves and one another or to fight back. In retrospect, this was only to be expected. "Would those who were taught to believe that Jews were subhuman admit in print to Jewish heroism?" Suhl asks.

The Jews did resist, heroically, though of all the European people who tried to fight the Nazis, they were the least able to do so, not only because they had been physically restrained and imprisoned behind ghetto walls almost from the beginning, or because they were systematically starved and subject to debilitating diseases, or even because they were the targets for the Nazis' maniacal murder plan. The Jews were least able to fight because they could not obtain weapons.

"The question of arms is the question without which resistance becomes mere rhetoric," Dawidowicz has noted. Scholar and analyst of Jewish history Abram L. Sachar has echoed this understanding. "The difference between resistance and submission," he wrote, "depended very largely on who was in possession of the arms that back up the will to do or die. The fact is that as soon as some of the Jews, even in the camps themselves, obtained possession of a weapon, however pathetically inadequate—a rifle, a knife, an ax, a sewer cover, a homemade bomb—they used it and often took Nazis with them to death." Joseph Goebbels himself, Hitler's propaganda chief, acknowledged this in the often-quoted backhanded compliment he paid to the Jews of the Warsaw ghetto. "The joke [the fighting] cannot go on much longer," he wrote, "but it shows what the Jews are capable of, when they have arms." In fact, the Warsaw Ghetto Uprising was the first mass open rebellion against the Nazis on the European continent, and it took the Nazis longer to defeat the ghetto fighters than it did for them to overrun all of Poland.

The story of Jewish resistance was not found in Nazi records, but it was found, bit by bit, piece by piece, when the war was over in the unofficial records written by the subjects of the Holocaust themselves, the people who had been its victims and its intended victims. From one end of Europe to the other, throughout the years of Nazi rule, individual Jews kept records of their own: diaries, journals, letters that could not be mailed, reports to underground groups, minutes of meetings of secret organizations, day-by-day accounts of life in the ghettoes, in the underground and in the resistance. People wrote because they sensed the enormity of what they were witnessing, the unprecedented and unbelievable events that were taking place. They realized that they themselves might well be doomed, and that in fact there might be no one left alive to tell the story. They wrote so that there would be a true record of their days, of what they had suffered, how they had struggled and how they had died. They hid their writings, gave them to trusted friends, buried them in the ground, threw them from trains in the hope that someday, someone would find them and learn the truth about what had happened, dignify their deaths with remembrance, honor them with mourning. The writings themselves were a way of fighting back, a gesture against oblivion, a refusal to vanish silently from the earth.

"I regard it as a sacred task," wrote one leader in the Warsaw ghetto, "for everyone to write down everything that he has witnessed or has heard from those who have witnessed the atrocities which the barbarians committed in every Jewish town. When the time will come—and indeed it will surely come—let the world read and know what the murderers perpetrated. This will be the richest material for the mourner when he writes the elegy for the present time. This will be the most powerful subject matter for the avenger."

In Warsaw, reports were collected in boxes that were hermetically sealed and buried in the ground. "My work was primitive," wrote one nineteen-year-old, "consisting of packing and hiding the material. . . . We used to say while working: we can die in peace. We have bequeathed and safeguarded our rich heritage. We reckoned that we were creating a chapter of history and that was more important than several lives. . . . What we could not cry out to the world, we buried in the ground. May this treasure be delivered into good hands, may it live to see better times, so that it can alert the world to what happened in the twentieth century."

The most extraordinary record was found at Auschwitz, created by the prisoners who were forced to remove the corpses from the gas chambers and place them in the crematorium. These eyewitnesses knew that they themselves would be gassed before long. They wrote accounts of the things they had seen and buried them in the ashes that covered the ground. "Dear finder," began one account, "search everywhere, in every inch of ground. Dozens of documents are buried beneath it, mine and those of other persons, which will throw light on everything that happened here. Great quantities of teeth are also buried here. It was we, the commando workers, who deliberately strewed them all over the ground, as many as we could, so that the world would find material traces of the millions of murdered people. We ourselves have lost hope of being able to live to see the moment of liberation."

Today, because of records left by the people who died, as well as the accounts of survivors, we know that in all the German-occupied lands of Europe and in the heartland of Germany itself, Jewish women and men fought back. In the forests of Eastern Europe, there were almost 20,000 Jewish partisans who disrupted the Nazi war machine in every way they could, with weapons when they had them, without weapons when they had none. They ambushed German troops, dynamited trains, wrecked communication lines. This song, "Zog Nit Keinmol" (Never Say), which used the melody of a Russian folk song and words by partisan Hirsch Glik, is known as the Hymn of the Jewish Partisans.

> Never say that there is only death for you,
> Though leaden skies have been concealing days of blue,
> The time is coming, yes the time is very near,
> Beneath our tread the earth shall tremble,
> "We are here!"

This song was written with our blood and not with lead.
It's not a song that summer birds sing overhead.
It was a people among toppling barricades,
That sang this song of ours with pistols and grenades.

From land of palm trees to the far off land of snow,
We shall be coming with our torment and our woe,
And everywhere our blood has sunk into the earth,
Shall our bravery, our vigor blossom forth.

So never say that there is only death for you.
Though leaden skies have been concealing days of blue,
The time is coming, yes the time is very near,
Beneath our tread the earth shall tremble, "We are here!"

In every ghetto too there was an underground. Most people have heard of the Warsaw Ghetto Uprising, but do not realize that there were underground fighting organizations and uprisings in almost every ghetto in Europe. In many, the people could not obtain any weapons at all. When the Nazis came for the people of the Lachwa ghetto, for example, the people attacked them with axes, knives and hammers—anything that could strike a death blow. Of the 2,000 Jews of Lachwa, about 100 survived the uprising and escaped to the forest where they joined the partisans. The people of the Bialystok ghetto, with twenty-five rifles, one machine gun and a few dozen hand grenades held off German tanks and armored cars for four days before they were overcome. The last words of Mordecai Tenenbaum, leader of the Bialystok resistance movement, were said to have been: "Jews! We have no arms! Grab sticks! Set fire to the houses!" They were all killed. "Even if we are too weak to defend our lives," read a declaration posted by the Bialystok resistance organization, "we are strong enough to defend our Jewish honor and human dignity, and thus prove to the world that we are captive but not defeated." Miles away, in the Otwock ghetto, Kalman Liss wrote a poem he entitled "I Sing the Song of the Blossoming Faith."

The autumn is menacing with rain
angry winds and icy gales,
but my song leaps like a brown antelope
over the path
bearing a promise of freedom to the world.

When one imagines the gruesome conditions in which the Jews were living, and the enormity of the power pitted against them, one must agree with Hungarian-born writer Elie Wiesel that "the question is not why all the Jews did not fight, but how so many of them did. Tormented, beaten, starved, where did they find the strength—spiritual and physical—to resist?"

Even in the death camps, the prisoners—the starving "living skeletons"—tried to stand up to their murderers. In a full-scale revolt in August 1943, inmates set Treblinka death camp on fire. Of the 700 prisoners who took part in the revolt, 500 were shot while still in the camp. Of the 200 who escaped to the woods, twelve eluded the reinforcements sent after them and survived. All 600 inmates of the Sobibor death camp revolted in October 1943. Over sixty survived the escape that followed. The German High Command considered the revolt so humiliating that it ordered the camp destroyed. These revolts, Yuri Suhl noted, "rank among the most dramatic narratives in the annals of the human struggle for survival." There was even an underground at Auschwitz, where twenty-one-year-old Rosa Robota's smuggling operation enabled inmates to blow up one of the crematoria. Rosa was later arrested and sentenced to death. Noah Zabladowicz, another member of the Auschwitz underground, made his way to Rosa's cell for a secret last visit. "When I became accustomed to the dark," he reported, "I noticed a figure, wrapped in torn clothing, lying on the cold cement floor. She turned her head toward me. I hardly recognized her. After several minutes of silence she began to speak. She told me of the sadistic methods the Germans employ during interrogation. It is impossible for human beings to endure them. She told me that she took all the blame upon herself and that she would be the last to go.

She had betrayed no one. I tried to console her but she would not listen.

" 'I know what I have done, and what I am to expect,' she said. She asked that the comrades continue with their work. 'It is easier to die when one knows that the work is being carried on.' "

Just before Noah left her cell, Rosa gave him a note on which she had written a message to her underground comrades. It was the greeting they used in their Zionist group. *"Hazak v'ematz,"* it said. "Be strong and brave."

The parachutists from Palestine were a small band, a whisper of defiance against the roaring forces of death in Europe. Like the fighters in the ghettoes and the rebels in the death camps, their chances for success were very small. Perhaps there was no chance at all. But they were there. They came to help, the only group from outside Europe that did. Arriving on a death-drenched continent, they represented life. At a time when the bonds between people were betrayed in ways more cruel than can be comprehended, the bonds they felt held fast. "We go out to our brothers in exile," Hannah had written while on her way back to Hungary. "Our hearts will bring tidings of springtime, our lips sing the song of light."

In all, 240 parachutists were trained by the British for the rescue mission. Thirty-two were dropped into the Balkans of Eastern Europe. Seven were killed: Abba Berdichev, Peretz Goldstein, Zvi Ben Jacob, Chaviva Reik, Rafael Reis, Enzo Sereni, and Hannah, "wonderful, sparkling Hannah," twenty-three years old, executed on November 7, 1944, by an irregular firing squad in the yard of the Margit Boulevard Prison. In another age, she might have been a poet.

The Nazi regime showed the world the monstrous capacities within the human heart, realities about human nature from which we are still recoiling in horror. The men and women who defied them show us that love and honor, courage and compassion are real too. Most of them, like Hannah, were killed, but their spirit was never overcome. Their love, their loyalty, their will to resist

*In 1950, Hannah's body was brought to Israel where
she was buried, with full military honors, in Haifa.*

was neither destroyed nor diminished. Their stories reach out to
us and bear witness to the reality of goodness. They give us hope
for our lives, the heart to struggle for one another's sake, the will
to leave our own good imprint on a world in which both the
worst and the best are possible.

"There are stars whose radiance is visible on earth though
they have long been extinct," Hannah wrote once. "There are
people whose brilliance continues to light the world though they
are no longer among the living. These lights are particularly
bright when the night is dark. They light the way for human-
kind."

Suggestions for Further Reading

Dawidowicz, Lucy S. *A Holocaust Reader*. New York: Behrman House, 1976.

Dawidowicz, Lucy S. *The War Against the Jews 1933–1945*. New York: Holt, Rinehart and Winston, 1975. (Young reader's version: Altschuler, David A. and Dawidowicz, Lucy S. *Hitler's War Against the Jews*. New York: Behrman House, 1978.)

Elon, Amos. *Understanding Israel*. New York: Behrman House, 1976.

Fein, Helen. *Accounting for Genocide: National Responses and Jewish Victimization During the Holocaust*. New York: The Free Press, 1979.

Gager, John G. *The Origins of Anti-Semitism*. New York: Oxford University Press, 1983.

Hoffman, Judy. *Joseph and Me in the Days of the Holocaust*. New York: KTAV Publishers, 1979.*

Lacquer, Walter. *A History of Zionism*. New York: Schocken Books, 1972.

*For young children, but moving and informative for young adults and adults as well.

Levin, Nora. *The Holocaust: The Destruction of European Jewry 1933–1945.* New York: Schocken Books, 1973.

Masters, Anthony. *The Summer That Bled.* New York: Washington Square Press, 1974.

Meltzer, Milton. *Never to Forget: The Jews of the Holocaust.* New York: Harper & Row, 1976.

Rosenbaum, Irving J. *The Holocaust and Halakhah.* New York: KTAV Publishers, 1976.

Sachar, Abram. *The Redemption of the Unwanted.* New York: St. Martin's Press, 1983.

Senesh, Hannah. *Hannah Senesh: Her Life and Diary.* New York: Schocken Books, 1973.

Suhl, Yuri. *They Fought Back: The Story of the Jewish Resistance in Nazi Europe.* New York: Schocken Books, 1967.

Syrkin, Marie. *Blessed is the Match: The Story of Jewish Resistance.* Philadelphia: The Jewish Publication Society of America, 1980.

Vital, David. *The Origins of Zionism.* New York: Oxford University Press, 1975

Index

agricultural school, Nahalal, Palestine, 44, *68, 71;* life at, 50–52, *50, 51*

Allied governments, and slaughter of Jews, 196–199

Anielewicz, Mordecai, 107–108

anti-Semitism, 3, 23–24, 36–39; in Hungary, 3, 4, 6–7, 9, 26–27; Hannah and, 9, 15–16, 18–19, 26–27, 43; Hitler and, 21–24; German, *22;* indoctrination of children, *25*

Armia Krajowa, 106

arms, availability of to Jews, 200

Arrow Cross Party, 30, 166, 169, 178, 179, 195

assimilation of Jews in Hungary, 4, 7

Astir, 56

Auschwitz death camp, 161, 163, *169;* records at, 202; underground in, 204

Austria, German takeover of, 20

Baden-Baden, synagogue burned, *34*

Balfour Declaration, 40

Battle of Britain, 67

Berdichev, Abba, 1, 124, 126, 205

Berlin, Jews attacked in, 33–34, *33*

Bialik, Nahum, 38

Bialystok ghetto, 203

Biela-Voda, Hungary, vacation in, 29–30

"Blessed is the Match," H. Senesh, 136

blitzkrieg, 65, 77, *91*

board game for children, *25*

Brandt, Gestapo chief, 103

Braverman, Sarah, 112

Budapest, Hungary, *2, 3, 3–4;* German soldiers in, *128;* Allied bombing of, 183, *184;* Russian advance on, 185

Buffum, David, 33

Caesarea, 84, *85,* 87, 97–99, *100*

Cairo, Egypt, rescue mission group in, 122–125

Chamberlain, Houston Stewart, 23

Chelmno death camp, 89

children: indoctrination of, *25;* Polish Jewish, *91*